D0065046
Suzanne
All hats
custom made

Putti
FINE FURNISHINGS

Although they were speaking in the immediate aftermath of the terrorist attacks on the World Trade Center and Pentagon on September 11, 2001, they were optimistic about the future.

If you think this might be the life you want and are considering opening a shop, you'll want to strike the right balance between preparing so much that you lose momentum or miss out on location or timing opportunities, and rushing in before you have taken the steps necessary for success. Some of those steps, such as retail experience in a shop similar to the one you plan to open, are optional, though advisable. Others, such as deciding on your merchandise, how you will arrange and package it, and how you will decorate your space, are what the enterprise is all about. Good business practices, such as keeping records and managing your finances, aren't lovable, and it's tempting to neglect them, but they *are* vital for success.

Ideas and inspiration for all these decisions abound in these pages, in the words of women who have already experienced and dealt with them. Starting you on the right path is an important goal of *A Shop of One's Own*. You are about to enter a stimulating new world. There may be bumps along the way, but if you are like the women in these pages, you will learn from them and go on to the next challenge. Welcome to what you were meant to do.

Linda Wade and her husband opened Putti Fine Furnishings in Toronto when their home began to overflow with their personal antiques collections. The name of the shop is a nod to Linda's special passion, cherubs.

GETTING STARTED

Just because you're passionate about having a shop of your own doesn't mean that starting a business isn't serious business. Although many of the women interviewed for this book say they are happy they "took the plunge" and "dived right into" shop ownership, a fair number said they began with insufficient funds and still stay up at night worrying about the financial health of their business. Undercapitalization is the major

OPE
ANTIQU

reason for business failure. Start-up costs are extensive—renting or buying space, purchasing merchandise, and paying for utilities, in addition to living expenses. The most likely sources of start-up capital are personal savings, the resources of family or friends, and a bank that knows you.

Legal Considerations

There are five basic forms a business can take, each with its own pros and cons. Before deciding which is best for you, be sure to discuss your particular situation with a financial adviser and a business lawyer, as not all of the legal entities described below may be available in your state or they may have different restrictions or requirements. The Small Business Association (SBA), which offers free classes, lectures, and online information, is a good source of reliable information.

Most of the businesses profiled in this book, and most businesses in the country, are operated as sole proprietorships, by far the easiest and the cheapest legal form a business can take. They are owned completely by one person, with no legal distinction between the individual and the business. This means the owner receives all profits, which are then reported on the owner's personal income tax return. It also means that

Shirley Maiden, who sells vintage clothing and new retro clothing made from old fabrics, and Judy Pascal, who sells antique furniture and accessories, share space in Manchester, Vermont. Although the women aren't business partners, their similar tastes and work ethic make it easy for them to function effectively as a collective.

the owner is personally liable for all debts and lawsuits.

A partnership is the association of two or more co-owners. Many women feel more comfortable starting a business with a partner because it's less overwhelming, and the partners can pool their strengths and finances to help the business grow. The drawback, as with a sole proprietorship, is that all owners are personally liable for any debts or losses the business incurs.

Almost half of all partnerships break up after one to three years because of business disputes, which is why business lawyers always recommend drafting a partnership agreement, even when

LESSONS

Finding Support

Neva Scott of Richland, Washington, decided on a Monday that she wanted to give up her job in real estate and open a shop selling cottage furniture and custom-painted pieces. She signed a lease that Wednesday. On Friday at dinner she asked her husband and teenage children if they wanted to help her clean out her desk. "No one stopped chewing," Neva recalls. The family celebration she had been expecting wasn't about to happen. After everyone was in bed, she took her personal business files to the banks of the Columbia River. Beginning at 3:00 A.M. she watched the paper from her fifteen years in real estate burn. It was still burning when the sun came up. When she arrived home five hours later, her family was paying attention. Neva opened Nest Feathers two weeks later with the full support of her family.

co-owners are family or friends. Although a partnership can be created verbally and informally, a formal contract outlining the responsibilities of each partner helps the partners plan for the most important issues in the business. This agreement can deal with topics such as how much time or money the partners will contribute, how decisions will be made, how profits or losses will be shared, how much vacation time or sick leave partners will have, what each partner's responsibilities will be, and what happens when one partner becomes ill, dies, or wants to dissolve the partnership.

A corporation is a more complex legal form and is therefore more expensive to establish and more complicated to operate. In order for a business to incorporate, it must issue company stock, which can then be bought and sold by the owners. Corporations usually have more than one owner, but individual business owners occasionally find it beneficial to incorporate and then buy 100 percent of the corporation themselves. The corporation is treated as a legal entity distinct from its owners. This distinction leads to the biggest advantage offered by a corporation: Shareholders are not personally liable for the debts the business may incur. And because the business isn't dependent on the owners, it can continue to exist even if one of the owners falls ill, dies, or sells all her shares. One of the disadvantages is the "double tax": The corporation must pay taxes on all profits, and then the shareholders must pay taxes on any dividends paid to them from these profits.

Many businesses avoid the problem of the double tax by filing as an S corporation. This allows the corporation to be treated like a partnership for tax purposes. This means that any profits flow directly to the shareholders' personal income tax return and there is no corporate tax. Not all states, however, recognize an S corporation, and there are many requirements to meet before a business can qualify for this status.

Another relatively new legal entity is the limited liability company, or LLC. This is similar to a corporation in that owners have limited liability if the business acquires debt, but it also allows the income to flow through to the owners' personal income tax returns, which means that owners are taxed only once. LLCs are, however, quite complicated and expensive to form.

Government Regulation

Government involvement in a new business takes many forms. Your state will issue a resale certificate and a resale number to let you buy wholesale without paying sales tax. You will become a tax-collecting arm of the government once you begin remitting the sales tax your customers are paying. If you hire employees, you will need an IRS-generated Employer Identification Number and will be responsible for withholding federal, state, and

"The name of the shop comes from my love of the outdoors—and the furniture I create, which brings the outside in," says Candy Rasmussen of Outside Inn in Redondo Beach, California. Her romantic hand-painted pieces can turn any room into a veritable indoor garden.

local income taxes from salaries, contributing to unemployment and workers' compensation systems, and matching the Social Security contributions you withhold from salaries as required by the Federal Insurance Contributions Act (FICA). If the name of your business is different from your own, you may, depending on where you live, have to register it with the county clerk and publish it in a local newspaper.

FAMILY INVOLVEMENT

Some families help with financing. Others lend special expertise such as decorating or accounting. Family members who are actively involved in the shop can make it more interesting.

At Ta Da!, Rosie Daykin's mother (pictured below with Rosie) works in the Vancouver gift and children's shop every day, drawing a salary. Rosie describes the relationship: "Mum views this as my thing, and she does it to help me out. I can't imagine anyone I'd trust more, but you want to be really, really sure before you do this. If anything is going to suffer, it'll be the relationship, not the business."

Linda Campisano Millinery has the benefit of Linda's businessman husband as a macromanager. He has always been encouraging and supportive of her entrepreneurial aspirations. Now he oversees the management of the downtown Chicago store, does interviews, and sets the pay scale, bringing a detachment that Linda feels her business needs but that she can't supply.

Keeping Records

Federal and state regulations and good financial management require good records. A bookkeeper or accountant can help you set up a ledger for keeping track of your shop's revenues and expenses. The same accountant should probably check for errors at the end of the year. You may also want to look into a record-keeping computer software program.

One excellent reason to keep good records is that small businesses, especially sole proprietorships, are favorite targets for IRS auditors. Expenses taken as deductions are an especially gray area. As a general rule, to qualify as legitimate deductions, expenses must be both "ordinary" and "necessary"—that is, they must be both common and accepted as well as appropriate and related to the business. Deductions for a home office where you have a separate shop can also be problematic.

By tracking sales, cash flow, and inventory, good record keeping also lets you make informed reordering decisions and profit-and-loss calculations. It gives you a clear picture of the state of your business and allows you to be in control of all aspects of it.

Establishing Credit

Imagine your business without credit: You'd have to pay COD—the full price in cash or check on delivery—for all merchandise and supplies. That's impractical and inconvenient, to say the least.

Business credit cards are an option, but even in the twenty-first century, plastic poses two major drawbacks: Some vendors won't accept it, and interest rates on credit card debt are high. Rhonda Eleish and Edie van Breems spent two years establishing a business credit history. Using personal assets as collateral, they obtained a one-year line of credit—a loan with a maximum payback period of one year—from a local bank and repaid it promptly. They also opened accounts with small vendors, such as fabric houses, and larger vendors, such as office supply chains, and paid them on time. This made it easy for their shop to open accounts on favorable terms with vendors and later to apply for bank loans.

Dealing With Vendors

Whether you encounter them manning a booth at the New York International Gift Fair, growing tulips in Holland, or crafting one-of-a-kind items in the American South, your vendors are a crucial factor in the success of your shop. When you ask a vendor for credit terms, you're beginning a relationship that is second in importance only to your relationships with customers. If the association is a good one, the vendor will tell you about exciting new items, warn you if a shipment is going to be late, and generally treat you as a favored customer.

The flowers at Flowers by Cecilia in Jackson Hole, Wyoming, stay beautiful for a long time because owner Cecilia Heffernan

QUICK TIP

Trade Credit

If you can show a vendor that you have a purchase order from a large company with a reputation for paying within 90 days, the vendor may carry you for that same period. With such generous terms, you are, in effect, borrowing from your vendors, or using "trade credit."

accepts only the freshest blooms from her suppliers, packed to preserve that freshness as long as possible. Growers respect her knowledge, and she has solidified her connections by visiting them herself when she can. Nina Kaplan of French Lace and Angel Heart in Newtown, Pennsylvania, also has had to be tough with vendors, but she knows she won't be able to sell an $800 pantsuit without a zipper, and she's not willing to supply what the manufacturer forgot.

Your role in a solid relationship means letting your vendors know how you're promoting their products. Maura Koutoujian of Henry's in Princeton, Wisconsin, showed the Argentinian maker of *dulce de leche* ("caramel to die for") how wonderful it looked on her web site, where she packages it with two antique silver spoons. She also sent them copies of *InStyle* magazine when that publication did a story on the holiday gift baskets she did for the cast of *Sex and the City*.

Some vendors shy away from businesses that are unknown to them or that deal only in small quantities of product. Photos of

DRIED COCONUT
DRIED CRANBERRIES
DRIED PEACHES

Buying a Business

In October 2000, Lorraine Eastman, owner of Beverly Flowers & Gifts, purchased Fraiche, a flower shop just across the street that was about to close. "I felt the products were too good and the following too big to let it fall off the map," she explains. Fraiche was gearing up for the Christmas holidays and preparing to implement a major new marketing plan, but the original owners had lost interest in the enterprise. While the shop was being overwhelmed with orders and inventory was running out, Lorraine, who had previously absorbed two other florists into her shop, was locked in negotiations with the seller. "Ours," she recalls, "was truly an eleventh-hour rescue. We saved the store in the nick of time."

Once the holiday rush was over, Lorraine invited magazine editors, neighboring shop owners, and clients, most of whom had never visited the shop (99 percent of the business is done by phone), to a party. She showed off the 2,000-square-foot space—a yellow exterior with an awning in the store's signature burgundy and a yellow and pale green interior with an island for assembling baskets—and introduced herself as Fraiche's new owner.

The typical Fraiche creation hasn't changed. It starts with a square-lidded hamper of grapevine or willow branches. Then it is filled with grade-one flawless fruit and a mixture of other delicacies—Swiss chocolates in natural wooden boxes, beauty products from Australia and New Zealand, soaps from France, and exotic coffees and teas are some of the possibilities. Baby baskets arrive with blankets and pillows, sterling silver rattles and cups, and teddy bears. The finished look is clean and elegant; no filler or cellophane uses up precious basket space. Lorraine added flower baskets to the offerings and has put a greater emphasis on personalized service.

With the experience of acquiring three different businesses, Lorraine has developed an invaluable list of tips about buying an existing enterprise: Research all aspects of the business; make sure employees understand your way of doing things; keep a vigilant eye on all expenses; and perhaps most important, beware of overexpanding.

your shop, information on your trend-setting customers and your infrequent markdown policy, and your popularity with magazine stylists—backed by photos and credits to prove it—can all strengthen your case.

Small foreign suppliers may be particularly difficult to work with. Linda Wade of Putti Fine Furnishings in Toronto signs up reluctant European makers by promising to sell their wares in cases bearing their name and by buying enough merchandise to make sure customers notice. If you don't have expertise dealing with vendors abroad, you may need to hire an agent in that country who speaks the language and can arrange letters of credit at a local bank to facilitate payment if your credit card isn't acceptable.

Of course, both sides should agree in advance on the terms of a sale. Always ask who pays for shipping, what the charges will be, where the shipping begins, who is responsible if purchases are damaged during shipment. Eileen Main of Farmhouse in Bennington, Vermont, found she could save money by picking up items from nearby warehouses. If you're paying the freight, indicate that you won't accept partial shipments, which multiply freight charges, and specify a cancellation date after which you won't accept the order. Get it in writing by issuing a purchase order.

If on occasion you can't meet a vendor's established terms—not unusual for a small shop—it's important to warn her that payment will be late, explain why, and detail the steps you are taking to improve the situation. When Pamela Scurry of Wicker Garden in New York City was in this position, she paid "every vendor a little bit every week with a little love note saying 'more to follow.'" Many vendors will reward a small entrepreneur's good credit history by extending payment terms over a longer period. "If you build a relationship in good times, it will last in bad," says Chicago milliner Linda Campisano.

QUICK TIP

Sunshine on the Side

Research shows that retail space is more productive if potential customers pass it going home rather than going to work and if it gets shade rather than sun in the afternoon.

Most small shop owners are reluctant to ask their sources for price reductions. Nest Feathers' Neva Scott feels that doing so is insulting to the home furnishings manufacturers and artists whose wares she sells. Other shop owners say they won't ask of vendors what they don't appreciate customers asking of them. As Carolyn Busch, who sells panama hats at Fino Fino in Menlo Park, California, puts it, "I never negotiate price with a hatmaker. I ask the price, and if I can sell it, I buy it."

WILD THYME
INC.
flowers
OPEN

FINDING A SPACE

According to the old adage, the three most important factors in retail and real estate are location, location, location. Beth Sisqueland-Gresch chose to locate Grasmere, her antiques and flower shop, in Barrington, Rhode Island, because she guessed that a small community, not too far from Providence and Boston's suburbs, would give her a better chance than a more cosmopolitan area for the gradual growth she wanted. Florist Laurie deGrazia of Wild Thyme wanted to locate between Wilmington and Philadelphia, convenient to the social-register families she saw as her primary customers. Rhonda Eleish and Edie van Breems were looking for space in Westport, Connecticut, when they found the perfect house for their eponymous antiques shop in nearby Woodbury and realized that a location in the "Antiques Capital of Connecticut" was what they wanted. Devonia's Lori Hedtler was willing to take a second-floor space for selling her antique and vintage tableware so she could afford the rent on Boston's chic Charles Street. And Eileen Main knew it was time to move when her Bennington location became too touristy for the sophisticated papers and gifts she was stocking. "A good lawyer made moving easy by inserting a clause in our lease saying that if business wasn't as good as we wanted it to be, we could leave in thirty days," Eileen notes.

Laurie deGrazia strategically set her flower shop on a scenic, much-traveled road between Philadelphia and Wilmington, Delaware. She's also close to a greenhouse and a 1,000-acre farm that serves as her cutting garden. Both are on land that has been in her family for several generations.

Once you decide to take a space, you may be able to ease your rent burden by volunteering to do the renovations yourself. One of Linda Campisano's Chicago-area landlords halved the rent for a desirable space when he learned she was willing to do the work herself. You may also be able to negotiate unequal payments, with smaller ones at the beginning of the lease, or a reduction in the security deposit. Be wary, however, of a landlord who is too willing to negotiate. Some locations seem to have a history of failure, and you certainly don't want to be in one of them.

NEGOTIATING

As CEO of Papyrus, a group of one hundred forty company-owned and franchise shops selling personalized stationery, greeting cards, and other paper and gift-related merchandise, Dominique Schurman is often involved in negotiations. She advises beginning with the understanding that you are looking for the point at which both sides will feel comfortable but warns that this balance is unlikely to be found in the absence of "fundamental trust." She also says it is important to know your boundaries, even to the point of writing them down, and not to get so caught up in the moment that you extend yourself beyond them. The essence of negotiating, Dominique has learned, is to give in areas where you have flexibility and to trade hard in areas where you don't. "Remember," she says, "there are always other

QUICK TIPS

Location Checklist

1. Would I want to spend time in the area?
2. Are the people who regularly come to the area likely to become my customers?
3. What attractions does the locale have already?
4. Are the nearby spaces rented? For how long? Would my shop be isolated?
5. Is it near public transportation, highways, and/or parking?
6. Are there any zoning restrictions—hours, signage and lighting, parking, or outdoor activities such as selling from the sidewalk—that might make it difficult to succeed?
7. For security considerations, is the space easily visible?
8. Do I have any other location options?
9. Can I create the feeling I want without a major transformation?
10. Is there room to store my merchandise? To have an office off the selling floor?
11. Can I fill the space without spending more than I can afford?
12. How long is the lease? Are there renewal terms? Is there a holdover clause?
13. Is there a clause covering business interruptions—if business is slow; if competition opens or a nearby major attraction leaves?
14. What will I have to pay in addition to rent?
15. Is there a nondisturbance clause saying that I can't be forced to move or sign a new lease if the building is sold or undergoes foreclosure?
16. If my renovation makes the space more desirable, will I receive a rent decrease? Will I have to return the space to its original condition before I leave?

THE SMART STORE

Regardless of the product you're selling, it's always smart to create an environment that will make your customers want to linger.

- Leave enough space between display tables and among items so customers can browse comfortably.
- Use different levels for display. Be sure that items on lower levels are easily visible and that those on higher levels are easily reachable.
- Place the cash wrap where workers can keep an eye on the front door. Put enticing impulse items near the register.
- Provide a chair or two and some reading material for children, the elderly, and fidgety husbands.
- Childproof the store if your customers are youngsters.
- Provide a coat rack, bag check, and umbrella stand so customers can shop unencumbered.
- Consider providing beverages, candies, or cookies. Think about playing soft background music.
- Be sure the bathroom reflects the same level of cleanliness and attention to detail as the rest of the shop.
- Install adequate lighting and mirrors that are flattering to your merchandise and your customers.
- Word your return policy graciously, then post it in an easy-to-see spot.
- List your hours prominently on the door.

GOOD DOG
UNDRY 15¢

opportunities, so be prepared to walk away if your negotiating partner doesn't give you what you need."

Security

The right location is probably the best precaution against theft, followed closely by carrying merchandise that is more valuable as a mark of taste than as stolen property on the street. A space without hiding places, plus neighbors who will look out for each other, are also helpful. Even with these factors in your favor, care is crucial. You want to avoid being either foolishly naïve or insultingly suspicious. As Maura Koutoujian of Henry's General Store in Princeton, Wisconsin, says, "I'd like to have hidden cameras, but I don't want to offend my affluent customers." She solves the problem, as most shop owners do, by being friendly, making eye contact, and "moseying over" whenever she sees a situation that might lead to trouble. All this must be done without hovering.

Arranging merchandise so that small, valuable pieces are easy for you to watch and difficult for customers to reach is a good precaution against theft. This may mean keeping them in a locked case, or perhaps locking the door and working by appointment. Elyssa Silbert often does this at Elyssa B Designs, her West Hollywood boutique built around the concept of customers actively handling a myriad of colored gemstones. If this kind of interaction isn't your main focus, you may decide that merchandise of this type isn't worth carrying.

LESSONS
Mistakes I Won't Make Again

1. Having no inexpensive items in my merchandise assortment.
2. Stocking too many small, valuable items, especially out of view of the main cash wrap.
3. Ordering items by the dozen for a small store where one-of-a-kind hand-picked merchandise is the main attraction.
4. Making the focus of the merchandise too narrow.
5. Letting suppliers push me around.
6. Selling from a space that doesn't allow outside signs.
7. Signing a lease before I know all the costs.
8. Renting raw space without access to inexpensive expertise about how to finish it.
9. Not charging for my consulting time outside the store.
10. Thinking I could duplicate the success of one highly personal shop when I opened another.
11. Using several personal credit cards to finance the business.
12. Promising special-order delivery dates without factoring in time for possible problems.

It also helps to have a tough reputation. Pamela Scurry, owner of Wicker Garden's Baby in Manhattan, says, "I'm not an easy target because I'm very aggressive about shoplifters. They know I'm going to get them locked up, so they try someone else."

Finally, if your space is sectioned and quirky and your wares are little and luxurious, you may have to consider an alarm system.

Shop owners suggest two ways of dealing with employee, or internal, theft. The first is to have policies in place that make stealing difficult. Tight management procedures, detailed records, extensive training, and daily bank deposits have all helped discourage shrinkage at the more than one hundred Papyrus shops. Dominique Schurman also makes unexpected visits to stores, which, she admits, "everyone hates," but she does because "they keep people on their toes."

The second is to institute policies that make stealing less appealing, such as profit sharing, generous employee discounts, and legal action when a theft has occurred. Michéle Rosier tries to reduce the problem at her Santa Monica flower shop by lending money to longtime employees, letting them buy store items at cost, and offering them a profit-sharing plan. But once a clear-cut case of theft arises, she goes straight to the local authorities. "There's no three-strike rule here," she says. "If they're stealing, they aren't just stealing from me but from others who have worked hard for their money as well."

INSURANCE

Insurance is a must, especially for a sole proprietor. A general guideline is that coverage should be complete but not overlapping, with the highest deductible you can afford. This will

Devonia's Lori Hedtler isn't worried about someone making off with one of the shop's vintage or antique plates. But she's decided not to include items with more obvious street value, such as sterling silver flatware, which might tempt would-be thieves.

mean lower premium payments. Comprehensive general liability insurance to protect you against negligence suits arising from accidents is also very important, as is a general business-insurance package covering theft of merchandise, equipment and fixtures, and damage from fire and water. Special situations require special insurance. If you take merchandise to trade or antiques shows, consider temporary coverage for any damages incurred outside your store. Automobile insurance should cover delivery drivers and vehicles. You may also want to consider health and life insurance on your staff and "key person" insurance on a partner.

Jen Stone of StoneKelly florists takes out a separate liability policy whenever she does floral decorations outside her Manhattan shop. This protects her against claims from clients, as well as injury claims by workers, who may be more prone to accidents in unfamiliar surroundings.

stonekelly

An Ideal Customer

Ta Da!

Rosie Daykin

Having worked for five years as an interior designer, Rosie Daykin of Vancouver, British Columbia, was ready and eager to directly express her own personal vision when she decided—in thirty seconds—to open a shop. Pragmatic and playful, she pushed up her timetable to take advantage of the "perfect" space when it suddenly became available. She opened her chic home, accessories, and children's clothing shop two months later, naming it Ta Da! ("That's vintage furniture speaking," Rosie explains. "After the refurbishment, it says, 'Ta Da!' ")

Luscious pink boxes and chocolate-brown ribbon signal that a delectable gift awaits. Owner Rosie Daykin knew from her years in the field of interior design that Vancouver residents would appreciate the unique mix of idiosyncratic objects she brings home from Paris and New York.

The shop is in a residential area that was becoming more commercially appealing: A grocery store had just become a café and a vintage clothing store was on the horizon.

ta da!
ta da!
ta da!
ta da!
3
4
PARIS
PARIS

Making use of every available space, Rosie attached a row of vintage doorknobs to a wall to display the tote bags she designs and has made locally (right). She splashed the shop's logo on store windows at eye level (above) so it's visible to drivers as well as pedestrians as they pass.

ta da!

Using carpenters and painters who had worked with her on design projects (which she still takes on for January and February, when the shop is quiet) and were willing to donate their services, she fixed up the 680-square-foot space that began life in 1910 as a beauty salon. She removed linoleum, painted the wood-paneled walls and floors white, and took down a false ceiling to expose the beautiful vintage tin behind it.

With a $20,000 line of credit from a local bank, Rosie assembled the merchandise that would bring the Parisian and New York style she loved to western Canada retailing. She fills the boutique with items she herself—her imaginary "ideal customer"—would want. She has added accessories, such as the "greatest handbag and the greatest mirror to go into it," which reflect her feminine taste in fashion, as well as pottery and tabletop pieces with an international sensibility—dishes and bistro tumblers from France and iced tea glasses from Morocco among them. She also designed a small selection of dresses and sweaters that "allow children to look like little girls instead of rock stars," with details such as pockets from embroidered handkerchiefs and buttoned-on aprons made from 1940s tablecloths that she has made up by local sewers and hand knitters. When she realized her ideal customer had nowhere to buy wonderful

Since her pre-opening budget didn't allow her to shop abroad, Rosie initially stocked the store with refurbished vintage pieces and new furniture made to her specifications. These might include unexpected pairings such as pillow ticking or white denim on ornate love seats and sofas.

nursery furniture, that, too, became a Ta Da! item, along with baby bath products from Italy and duck-handled umbrellas from France.

Ta Da! carries $5 books and $8 tassels as well as $3,000 sofas and $1,200 chandeliers because Rosie doesn't want anyone to say, "I can't afford anything in this store." Adding to the "unpretentious and unclubby" atmosphere in the shop is Rosie's "Mum," Pixie Porcellato. Rosie describes her as "an unbelievable person who can talk to people all day long and love it." But she warns others to think really hard before hiring a relative; mixing the personal and the professional can result in disaster—for the personal.

Rosie couldn't be happier that she overcame her initial doubts about making her personal vision so public. And she doesn't listen to the naysayers—"They may be negative because they don't want you to accomplish what they'd like to accomplish themselves," she says. "I don't mind if it doesn't work. It would have been more frustrating for me not to have tried it."

Judging from Rosie's customers, it's working just fine. Many are regulars who visit the shop on an almost daily basis to see how she has rearranged her wares. "People get it," she says with delight. "They appreciate this shop that I created from my head and may even say, 'This is the most beautiful store I've ever been in.'"

Rosie likes to feature items that can serve many purposes beyond the purely decorative. A cut-glass container can become a wine decanter or a vase for roses. A clear, fluted compote easily functions as a holder for napkins, note cards, or invitations.

CARTE POSTALE

Set Design

Eleish-van Breems Antiques

Rhonda Eleish and
Edie van Breems

ven before owners Rhonda Eleish and Edie van Breems have said, "Hi, how are you? Make yourself at home, and please let us know if we can help you," the welcome at their Swedish antiques shop in Woodbury, Connecticut, is warm and friendly. The greeting begins at the back of the shop, where a formal garden stretches out near the parking lot and a wooden deck with antique benches invites families to snack. It continues inside, where Rhonda and Edie encourage customers to "take off your shoes and lie down on the couch." To make sure there's something for everyone, the shop stocks $30,000 armoires as well as less expensive furniture made to their specifications in Tibro, Sweden's furniture reproduction capital. The store even welcomes children and will keep an eye on strollers

The Swedish flag flies outside the 1760 Thompson House shop in Woodbury, Connecticut, as a reflection of the owners' missionary zeal for Sweden's antiques and lifestyle.

(with or without passengers) if parents want to wander unencumbered from shop to shop in this antiques center of Connecticut. Men feel at home in the smoking room, which is decorated with hunt paintings and brightened by a roaring fire in the winter. Shoppers are offered fruit, gingerbread cookies, Swedish coffee, and exceptional chocolates. More formal entertainment includes a mother-daughter tea prepared by a Swedish chef and a thank-you cocktail party at Christmas.

It adds to the graciousness of the hospitality that all this occurs in a sun-filled house with wide plank floors and windows and ceilings that are unusually generous for its eighteenth-century origins. Rhonda noticed the property as the FOR SALE sign was going up. The partners had an instant rapport with the sellers that gave them the winning bid, but they didn't actually purchase the house until they had obtained a zoning variance that made a 50 percent–commercial space possible. Rhonda now lives on the second floor of the shop. The women spent four months painting and rewiring, installing alarm and stereo systems, and enlarging, then screening, the driveway for customer parking.

Because the Swedish government restricts furniture exports and forbids national treasures to leave the country, the shop also buys furniture in other European countries. Here a statue and orb, both French, beautifully complement the Swedish table and mirror.

The history of retail shops is filled with failed partnerships, but Rhonda and Edie's relationship has had staying power. It's based on a friendship that started in sixth grade and

became a new link in a chain their parents (who share a Swedish heritage and a love of antiques) had forged years earlier. Deciding to go into business seemed natural. After working together on charity projects, the women found they had "the same vision and concepts, even though we're very different people." It also helped that they brought a combined thirty years of preparation—

Rhonda and Edie work diligently to create complete room settings that show off both furniture and accessories to best advantage. A generous, inviting, and restful spirit pervades each room.

Rhonda was a merchandiser for a large women's clothing chain and a local antiques store, and Edie was a commercial photographer's agent.

A small canopy made of light and airy fabric such as muslin is typical of the Swedish Gustavian style (below). The Gripsholm armchair—a style that harks back to the same period—is actually part of the shop's reproduction line. Vintage pewter plates (opposite) are used when the owners entertain in-store.

The warmth the women feel for each other is part of the personality and charm of the store. "The shop has become a bit of a salon," Edie says. "We're as happy as little clams. People sense our enthusiasm and become part of our family."

Anandamali

CHERYL HAZAN

heryl Hazan was already a professional mosaic maker when Cecile Arnaud knocked on her door carrying a portfolio of the mosaic-covered furniture she had been selling in France. Cecile proposed that the women work together to create similar pieces for the U.S. market. Cheryl had been using a mosaic technique of her own invention to decorate hurricane lamps in her own forty-person factory. She was intrigued by Cecile's work, in which dishes and vases are broken into precisely shaped pieces, then rearranged according to a preset pattern to form a new design. The work is called picassiette (a combination of a shortened form of the name Picasso and the French word for plate). As Cecile began teaching her the technique, Cheryl realized it was time to

Anandamali's "around the world" chest, a prototype design, is a mosaic of blue and white plates, including English Blue Willow and Flow Blue, that evoke the sea. A stack of whole cups and saucers on top of the bureau is a witty counterpoint to the picassiette.

leave the world of manufacturing and return to the world of art, which had always been her passion.

The women became creative but not financial partners, says Cheryl, and are "perfectly in tune." They spent a year at flea markets collecting fifteen thousand plates and two thousand vases to be turned first into sample pieces and then into custom-made work for clients. In 1995, Cheryl opened Anandamali, a 2,000-square-foot gallery space with poured concrete floors and exposed ceiling pipes in the hip Tribeca section of lower Manhattan. The shop, which also showcases art and upholstered furniture from studios in the neighborhood, soon became a destination for home owners and designers looking for unusual pieces. The shop's name is as unique as the creations it displays: *Anandamali* is a Sanskrit word meaning "beautiful garland" and refers to the Tibetan custom of making personal garlands by adding a new flower for each new life experience. Cheryl and Cecile enhance the shop's eastern karma by serving tea and burning sandalwood incense.

Saucers turn into sideboards, creamers to cabinets, teapots to coffee tables—all as surface decoration. Once cast off by collectors for their chips and cracks, these ceramic bits now form the basis of beautiful new designs. "I'll often buy entire dinner sets from secondhand stores," Cheryl says, "but I have no use for large tureens or platters. If they match a piece of furniture a customer has chosen, I'll include them as a gift."

For owner Cheryl and "chief artisan" Cecile, a commission is a three-step process of reading the customer's fantasies, translating them into a pattern, and decorating the piece of furniture. They often form a friendship with the new owner, which they hope includes

"visitation rights" for pieces they have difficulty parting with. In a workshop behind the gallery, the women collaborate on plate selection and overall design and work together gluing the mosaic pieces to the bare furniture. In between these steps, trained helpers cut the plates. Although other artists employ a technique similar to picassiette when they use broken pottery to fashion random patterns on furniture, the precision of Cheryl and Cecile's creations makes their work unique in the United States.

Anandamali is often featured in home decorating magazines and on television shows. One year, their pieces were chosen as gifts for Polygram's recording stars, including Sting and Elton John.

Anandamali's styles can be funny or serious, modern or traditional, and vary in price depending on the rarity of the plates used to make the mosaics—a four-drawer chest made with Limoges plates, for example, is more expensive than a similar chest made from Blue Willow plates purchased at a garage sale. Individual pieces range from picture frames to armoires. Not long ago the women transformed a customer's Israeli plates into the wall and floor of a room for her Aspen home and shipped it to Colorado, where it was assembled like the pieces in a puzzle.

One of their most exciting commissions was to transform an entire Manhattan town house by creating a picassiette fireplace mantel, a four-wall kitchen backsplash, a "carpet" that looks like a kilim rug, and the walls of one bathroom.

The samples on display in the shop include a large round table with solid green, square tiles and round floral centers, a chest of drawers with bits of mirror embedded in an abstract design suggesting the Far East, and an antique chest designed around a hand-painted eighteenth-century plate that invokes the feminine garden scenes of Fragonard and Watteau.

In the summer, when things are quieter in New York City, the women give lessons in picassiette, using a kit and instruction book they developed. They have also started spending time at a new studio in Toulon, France, which allows them access to dishes not available in the United States.

Although Cheryl admits that starting the business was "excruciatingly difficult," she now sees that effort's blissful result. The playfulness of the work she creates with Cecile is enhanced by the other art in the gallery. Their Tribeca neighbors are friendly and helpful, and "everything goes together to create a beautiful harmony of spirit and joy."

There's more to see than first meets the eye: Porcelain marks and shards are on their way to becoming the kind of cabinet the complete set of china would once have been stored in (opposite, left). In a small area on a chest of drawers (opposite, right) are fragments from hundreds of Victorian medallion plates.

KEEPING EVERYONE HAPPY

Barefoot Contessa

INA GARTEN

Ina Garten's main requirement for the people she hires at Barefoot Contessa, her vibrant gourmet emporium in East Hampton, New York, is happiness. Ina, who in the 1970s went from doing budget analysis for nuclear regulatory policy in the White House to owning a prepared food and charcuterie shop on eastern Long Island, learned the hard way that a friendly, well-educated staff is a key ingredient in a successful retail enterprise. "It's a lot easier to teach someone how to recognize a ripe Brie than it is to turn a food expert into someone you'd want to share a meal with," she explains.

Barefoot Contessa's entrance resembles nothing so much as the front door of a home, conveying the store's welcoming ambience to shoppers even before they step inside.

Helping Ina achieve her goal of having customers come in for a baguette and leave with a basketful of goodies extends even further than her cordial staff. She does everything she

BAREFOOT
CONTESSA
fine foods

BAREFOOT CONTESSA
fine foods
STILTON
BAREFOOT CONTESSA
fine foods
ENGLISH
FARMHOUSE
CHEDDAR
BAREFOOT CONTESSA
fine foods
L'EDEL
$15.05 LB
46 Newtown Lane
East Hampton, New York
(516) 324-0240
L'EDEL
DE CLERON
L'EDEL
DE CLERON
CLERON
FRANCHE COMTE
cheBaron

can to convey the welcoming feeling of "coming home to Mom": Barefoot Contessa's incredibly aromatic coffee is out on a burner so customers can help themselves. Baked goods and breads are on twenty-five feet of tables, not in a locked case or behind a counter. At least six dips and breads are available for tasting. Flowers and high-energy "feel-good" music make the 3,000-square-foot black-and-white–tiled shop feel like a party every day.

If employees aren't adding to the pleasant and homey picture Ina wants to paint, she discusses with them how to improve. She allows a probationary period for change, but if their performance isn't better, she lets them go. She makes a point of explaining her decision to the rest of the staff so they are clear about her requirements. She always lets her employees know what is expected of them, showing consideration for their feelings by praising publicly and criticizing privately.

Staffers and customers alike soon catch on to the earthy yet elegant style connoted by the shop's name, which comes from a 1954 movie starring Ava Gardner and Humphrey Bogart. Quality is tops and flavors are bold. Ina believes that people should be able to tell what the food is going to taste like by looking at it. The store's signature brownies are dark and rich, with a hint of coffee flavor, and are slightly undercooked; mustard chicken

"Baked goods, breads, and cheese are on wooden tables like a dessert table in my home," says Ina, "instead of hidden away in a case or refrigerator." She donates food to local charitable events to raise money for the historical society and Planned Parenthood.

salad is yellow with mustard seeds, not powder. Ever the perfectionist, Ina even hired a consultant from New York's Metropolitan Museum of Art to demonstrate how lighting fixtures and green window shades could make already appealing food look as luscious as an Impressionist painting.

Since the shop makes its own breads, pastries, salads, vegetables, and main courses, the fifty employees can choose an area in which to specialize or move from section to section to keep their work interesting. Ina, who was only an amateur cook when she bought Barefoot Contessa, is able to do all the jobs herself, from chunking chicken to layering tarts to accounting, so, as she says, "No one in the store will own me." Her sense of independence extended to the shop's location, and soon after she moved in, she bought the brick building that houses the store.

Many years ago Ina began delegating serious responsibility to her top employees. Because she's often away scouting other shops and new products in this country and abroad, she has always relied on her staff to report customers' requests and complaints. Five years ago she began the ultimate delegation when she offered her chef and her manager the opportunity to acquire shares in Barefoot Contessa. Now the two own the shop, giving Ina the freedom to write two best-selling books as well as columns on cooking and entertaining. The books

A good marketer, Ina misses no opportunities to trumpet her shop's name throughout the store. Beautiful printed ribbons like regatta flags appear on prepackaged Barefoot Contessa candies.

have put the store on the map beyond the New York metropolitan area, and while this national reputation hasn't meant a rash of mail-order sales—except for coffee—it has made the locals in this celebrity-crammed spot on Long Island even more likely than before to buy their boeuf bourguignon and biscotti at Barefoot Contessa.

French General

MOLLY AND KAARI MENG

A few steps from the bustle of lower Manhattan's Chinatown, in a corner of cosmopolitan SoHo, is quiet Crosby Street. Next to a popular tapas bar and across the street from a new celebrity-filled apartment building, a simple sign announces FRENCH GENERAL, a one-of-a-kind store with a one-of-a-kind story. More than a decade earlier in Grandview-on-Hudson, just north of New York City, Kaari Meng began making jewelry from old glass beads she and her sister Molly found at flea markets in the South of France. Five years later they realized that the *bricolage* they were buying—unusual tape measures, old sequins and feathers, painted buttons—and the beads were as irresistible to friends in New York as they had been to them

The Meng sisters prowl around markets and hardware stores in France to find objects as diverse as vintage jewelry and ribbons (opposite), French soaps and fine candles, new children's shoes and old lunch boxes. "We're like an old-fashioned general store where you'd find anything from buttons to buckets," says Kaari.

French General
35 Crosby Street
YARD
No 212 343 7474
Feather Stitch
Feather Stitch
Warranted
490

one for me
one for me
one for you
160
54
40
RED-WINGED BLACKBIRD

in France. The sisters started selling out of a barn in Grandview a few days a month. Two years later they decided to combine the jewelry and *objets* businesses, add vintage textiles and linens to the mix, and take the whole enterprise into New York City.

Kaari and Molly were searching lower Manhattan for a space for the shop when a friend told them to try Crosby Street. They soon found the perfect spot in terms of location (within walking distance of their new home) and size (2,200 square feet). Despite the fact that it also came with black walls, purple chairs and tables—its last incarnation was as a bar—and cockroaches, they signed a lease in July of 1999.

Two days later, Kaari was diagnosed with cancer. The entire Meng family immediately came East from California and swung into action, transforming the space into an area suitable for retail. The girls' father and two brothers and Kaari's husband began painting walls, sanding floors, and redoing the bathroom. In Grandview, Molly, their mother, and their sister-in-law got merchandise ready as they kept Kaari company and nursed her through chemotherapy. This heroic effort, plus a landlord who relieved the pressure to succeed right away by making the rental an unusual month-to-month or year-to-year option, enabled French General to open in time for

Baubles and bibelots are displayed in old bureaus, which themselves may be on sale depending on the Mengs' mood and the "karma" of the piece. This optician's case is filled with items such as a vintage compact and cards and a new glass bracelet designed by Kaari.

Christmas that year. The girls' parents stayed to work on the selling floor, and returned to help out again the following year. These days Mr. and Mrs. Meng make two of the shop's four annual buying trips to France.

Outside the shop, a white bench announces French General's hospitality. The inside features one wall of exposed brick, another wall of French blue so popular with shoppers that a painter friend mixes it for sale in the store, and a curtain of red-and-white toile dividing the selling space from the office and jewelry workshop behind it. The old oak bar from the space's previous life is now white with a French blue stripe. It holds whatever is seasonal or new to the shop—blue-enameled measuring cups; a bracelet made from old glass black balls, tiny yellow lemons, and even smaller green leaves; soap for Valentine's Day; and handmade greeting cards—plus signature items such as Number Two pencils stamped with "French General" and toy soldiers in Napoleonic uniforms.

Innovative display ideas abound. The store's red leather tote bags are hung from the handlebars of a red tricycle, and ancient tea towels are stacked up in a vintage crib. Imported writing paper, soaps from a French factory that uses old molds, and fragrant candles—always lighted to cast a romantic glow around the shop—share space with ropes of buttons that might someday become a

Spools of brightly colored ribbon—some French, some American—are piled on an antique wooden table. "French people who discover us tell us the shop reminds them of their grandmother's house," says Molly.

E-Z WASH
WASH RESISTANT
RAYON
SEAM BINDING
WOVEN EDGE - 100 YDS.
MFD BY LAWRENCE SCHIFF SILK
BUSER
CORONET
Quality
BUSER
CORONET
NO. 40
10 YARDS
French General
INVENTORY GAUGE

necklace, a cast-iron frog that can be a bookend or doorstop, feathers that might form a wreath or adorn a hat.

Not everything is from France, however—things are just "generally French at French General," as Kaari puts it. Mixed in with the vintage French items are early American dolls and games, ironstone dishes, and fine writing papers.

French General is the epitome of hominess. Kaari and Molly love to chat with customers. They're always curious about how an item is going to be used by its new owners and are happy to give an object's whole history if they know it. "It's as if there's a ghost inside each old piece, talking to the customer who should own it," Molly says. Kaari adds, "It's good for us that the street doesn't get a lot of traffic, because when customers come in, we can spend time with them. We say hello to everyone. Some people stay for an hour."

The Meng sisters have such a good eye for appealing pieces that French General bibelots often appear at celebrity parties and in movies and magazines. This gives the store a steady source of both revenue and publicity, and it spreads the cozy feeling of the shop way beyond its Crosby Street home.

Enamel pails found in the cellars of hardware stores hold an assortment of colored sponges. The shop also carries scented soap, lavender body lotion, and vintage quilts for the shopper looking for a complete bed-and-bath experience.

Follow Your Instinct

Nest Feathers

Neva Scott

Neva Scott found her calling—dealing in fine furniture and furniture finds—when she decorated her daughter's college apartment. After thirteen years as a successful real estate agent, she quit her job. She scoured thrift shops, bought on consignment from a house sale, and raided her own home for cottage-style furniture and accessories. Two months later she opened her own shop, Nest Feathers in downtown Richland, Washington, a metropolis of 165,000. The 1,000-square-foot store is divided into three rooms, each a mix of refurbished, recycled, and custom-decorated pieces—a wood-canopied potting shed, a floral sofa upholstered to Neva's specifications, a distressed white table. Vintage upholstered pieces are usually redone in chintz, faded

Nest Feathers' artists will paint every type of furniture, from chairs and tables to mirrors and doll beds. The distressed white-painted bench, opposite, was actually made from the headboard of an old twin bed.

Nest Feathers

floral, or a combination of fabrics. Old-fashioned kitchen chairs, spruced up and repainted, line up against the walls. Little cabinets crafted from old pieces wait for new homes. Mirrors and clocks of different eras hang on the walls. Cream and white china fill shelves and tabletops.

In order to carry pieces that would attract designers from Seattle, one hundred fifty miles away, Neva knew she had to offer something unique. One day, she took unfinished chairs to local schools in search of students who might want to decorate them for a fee. As it turns out, none of the students got the work, but local artists heard about Neva's search and began to show up at her shop. Relying on her original idea, she gave each applicant a test chair. Although she usually knew right away which work would sell and which wouldn't, she put every chair on display and let the customers make the decision. The artists whose pieces sold have stayed with Nest Feathers, some since just after the store opened in 1997.

Neva now has eight artists working with the shop, ready to transform any piece a customer might bring in. Their backgrounds range from self-taught to degrees in fine arts. Their styles run the gamut from traditional decorative painting to the whimsical and fantastic. Some of the artists specialize in faux finishes, trompe l'oeil, and realistic and fanciful renderings of plants and animals. One, the shop's "wild woman," paints imaginative flowers and plants that Neva calls "vibrant and free-spirited."

The typical Nest Feathers customer is a woman between fifty and sixty-five. While all are drawn to the cottage style the shop promotes, some want to achieve it with new furniture, and others come in looking for vintage pieces from the 1930s and 1940s. Many are looking for a way to salvage a family heirloom they really don't like but feel guilty about hiding in the attic. "If you can imagine it, we can do it," says Neva. "We show

A dining room table painted by one of Neva's artists bursts with fresh-as-summer flowers, turning it into a one-of-a-kind piece.

different artists' work until we find the perfect solution. When we do, I've had people hug me and burst into tears."

Neva encourages her artists and takes particular care with their feelings. In the rare instance when a buyer is unsatisfied, she offers a refund and the artist is paid for her time. When clients are pleased, Neva is certain to pass on the compliment. She even takes her support of the arts a step further by letting her shop, located in the arts and entertainment district of gentrifying downtown Richland, serve as an informal box office for local performance companies that can't afford their own ticket-selling space.

Negotiating is not part of the culture at Nest Feathers. Neva believes strongly in paying people what they're asking. If she doesn't think a piece is worth the price, she goes somewhere else. "I know the upholsterer is giving me a good deal, and I don't degrade him by negotiating," she says.

Being a proprietor has been much less stressful for Neva than her years in real estate, where a client's loss of a job, a foreclosure, or a divorce meant that "really bad things were happening to people and you couldn't help them." Though decorating one's home is an important and emotional subject, she takes comfort in knowing that "nothing crucial hangs on a door or a table."

Birdhouses, displayed on pedestals made from old chair legs, table legs, and pepper mills and set out on a vintage bureau, are only one of Neva's favorite collectibles. She continually searches for little floral creamers, orphan teacups, and white pitchers of any description.

PLANNING FOR SUCCESS

Women who are passionate about owning a shop say their life isn't about money. However, business *is* about money, and being a successful retailer requires that expenses be carefully controlled. Three financial statements—cash flow, income, and balance sheet—help you keep track of and manage your business's financial health. They may not give you any information about your shop's potential for growth, its reputation in the community, or

LOULOU'S
LOST & FOUND
LUXURY WITH ECONOMY

the pleasure you derive from it, but they will provide you with an essential reality check.

At its most basic, a cash flow statement tracks all the money flowing into your business, from sales of your wares or services, and flowing out to pay for expenses, such as rent, insurance, utilities, and inventory. In its early stages, your business may not be generating much revenue, but you will still have expenses to cover; preparing a projected cash flow statement before you open your doors can help you estimate the amount of cash you'll need. Most experts suggest estimating expenses higher and revenues lower than you expect so that you have some flexibility should unforeseen expenses arise.

Once the business begins to operate, you can compare statements from month to month—and eventually year to year—to help you plan a cash flow strategy. This will help you weather the slow times and take advantage of the peak times. For example, when wedding work declines in the winter, Beth Sisqueland-Gresch of Grasmere in Barrington, Rhode Island, puts fresh flower sales on hold and turns to the business of decorating with dried flowers. At Flowers by Cecilia in Jackson Hole, Wyoming, Cecelia Heffernan buys plants, which are less perishable, for the winter season. In Vermont,

A handsome art deco logo previews what shoppers will find inside Boston's LouLou's. Vintage tableware, often put to unexpected and creative uses, might include a silver ice cream coupe from a French café used as a vase, and sherbet dishes holding tiny soaps.

Shirley Maiden, who sells vintage and reproduction vintage clothing at Maiden Lane in Manchester Center in the summer, cuts her expenses by closing the shop for a few weeks in the winter. During the break, she produces reproduction clothing to sell to other stores.

The income statement, also called the profit and loss statement or P&L, records the income generated and expenses incurred during a given period—a month, a quarter, or a year—and measures the amount of profit or loss over that period.

Gross profit is the total sales figure minus the cost of goods sold. To calculate the net profit or loss (before taxes), simply deduct all expenses—everything from rent, utilities, salaries, supplies, and professional services to advertising, packaging and shipping, insurance, and travel—from your gross profit. Many experts suggest that small business owners include their own salary in the total expenses to ensure that they at least cover their living expenses while the business is operating. A good way to determine an appropriate salary is to estimate what you would be making if you were working at a comparable job somewhere else.

The income statement can also function as a useful management tool. By highlighting problems, such as expenses that can be eliminated, it will help you define and plan your financial goals.

A balance sheet shows the financial position of a business at a specific point in time using a basic formula: total assets minus total

QUICK TIPS
Controlling Expenses

1. Negotiate hard for the best lease terms you can get.
2. Make necessities such as shopping bags and delivery vehicles do double duty as ads for your shop.
3. Buy inventory sparingly. This not only eliminates tying up too much money, it also signals to customers that supplies are limited—if they want it, they have to buy it now.
4. Regulate shop hours to reduce the cost of help.
5. Rearrange your merchandise instead of buying more.
6. Buy supplies in bulk if you have a place to store them.
7. Learn how to do simple repairs yourself.
8. Be good to your vendors; they may reward you with special deals.
9. Be knowledgeable about technology—a computerized system may put the cart before the horse.
10. See what membership in your local Chamber of Commerce offers in the way of services or marketing programs.

liabilities equals owner's equity. Assets include such items as cash, inventory, accounts receivable, and equipment. Liabilities include outstanding loans, accounts payable, and taxes. A negative equity figure indicates that the business is in a weak financial position.

Inventory

Inventory is the technical term for all those beautiful and blissful things that you plan to sell. Accurate record keeping, whether on computer or by hand, requires regular tracking of each item as it

The Christmas Season

A good Christmas can make a good year, so smart shop owners always plan some sort of holiday promotion. At Room with a View, a home decor and gift shop in Santa Monica, Elizabeth Lamont holds an open house the first Friday in December, with Dickens-style carolers, food and wine, and stories for children. She invites her vendors and reps as well as her loyal customers to the party. Grasmere, Beth Siqueland-Gresch's dried flower and floral event shop in Barrington, Rhode Island, makes the store itself festive by serving hot mulled cider and cookies and even providing live music on the premises several times between Thanksgiving and Christmas.

At Desana in Boston, Paula Goldstein gives her male customers a special night to come in and have a unique fragrance mixed for someone special in their lives. The store is open late, there are goodies for nibbling, and there are always noncustom items such as soaps, mirrors, and perfume bottles —good for men who don't go for all that sniffing.

Although she plans for Christmas all year, Linda Wade at Putti in Toronto says the holiday really begins October 31 when her staff transforms the large antiques and home furnishings shop into a wonderland of themed rooms. There are roses in the Rose Room and pastel ornaments in the Grey Room. Magnolia-and-boxwood wreaths are displayed on an antique sleigh on the sidewalk. Christmas music and candlelight help set the scene. Linda also sets up a big display promoting the store at an annual charity event called the Sugarplum Fair to benefit the Toronto Ballet School, and even decorates a few houses in over-the-top holiday finery.

For The McCharles House Restaurant, Tearoom and Gardens in Tustin, California, Christmas comes twice a year. Audrey and Vivian Heredia present "Christmas in July," a Victorian custom, and make it last the whole month. The food of summer, flavored with lots of rosemary and lavender, mixes with the decor and music of Christmas. There are evergreen branches, cinnamon cookies, St. Nicholas–blend tea—even little twinkly tea candles that almost make people forget that the other Christmas is almost half a year away.

QUICK TIPS
Before You Order

1. Which customers are likely to be interested in it?
2. What will your selling price be?
3. Would you buy it at the price you want to charge? Would you give it as a gift?
4. Where will you display it? Where will you move it if it doesn't sell quickly?
5. Does it stand on its own or does it need help from something else? Do you already have the "something else"?
6. Does it fill a hole in your merchandise offerings?
7. Is the supplier reliable?
8. Can you sell it next season if it doesn't sell this season?
9. Is this the best place to buy it? The best time? Is it returnable?
10. Who else is likely to be selling it in your area?

enters your shop (through purchases) and leaves (through sales). Periodically, you should take a physical inventory and actually touch and count all the merchandise on hand, or "in inventory." For many businesses, a logical time to do this is at the end of January, when Christmas sales and returns have been completed and the shop is relatively quiet.

Keeping track of your merchandise on a regular basis helps you reorder and restock popular items, alerts you to the possible need for price reductions on slow-moving pieces, and allows you to see where shrinkage (theft) might be occurring. There are several excellent computer programs on the market to help you track and record pertinent information, such as item names and code numbers, vendor names, and contact numbers.

Desana's Paula Goldstein uses the Japanese system of just-in-time inventory, in which a business avoids tying up money in inventory by purchasing in small quantities and carrying only the amount of merchandise it can sell in a short period. She can get ingredients for her custom fragrances

At Farmhouse, Eileen Main never buys more than six of any one item, then puts her total inventory on display. Alert shoppers know that if they see something they like, "it's now or never." She artfully mixes craft pieces such as stuffed animals with gardening tools and cocktail napkins, affixing a store label to everything to discourage imitation by competitors.

Choosing the Mix

Linda Getchell found the right mix of merchandise for her eclectic boutique through trial and error. Getchell's, located in the tony southwest quadrant of Minneapolis, is furnished with oriental rugs, oil paintings, antiques, and her collections of 750 vases and 2,000 vintage fabric panels, all for sale. In the early 1990s, as a response to economic hard times, Linda broadened her merchandise choices to include luxury soaps and candles as well as antiques. "The people who can no longer afford antiques are now loyal gift buyers," she explains.

Linda's name is on the outside of the shop because her seal of approval is on everything inside it. Each item is there for a personal reason. The French soap has been selected not only because it smells wonderful, but also because it doesn't stimulate Linda's allergies. The ice cream topping and artichoke dip are her children's favorites. The CDs were handpicked by her son. The books were read by her daughter's book club of 28- to 35-year-olds or by Linda's friends' club of 45- to 55-year-old women. She personally vouches for the efficacy of the home care products she carries. The shop's jewelry is made by a friend who mixes vintage beads with pieces from estate sales and auctions.

Although the shop's selective philosophy reduces the possibility of excess inventory, Linda still had to learn from experience that buying by the dozens wasn't right. Now she buys only what she's passionate about. "If soap or body lotion comes in seven fragrances, I pick what I personally use on a regular basis. I buy enough so it doesn't look skimpy on the shelf, but not so much that it looks like overkill."

quickly, so this system works well for her. At Eleish-van Breems, the owners know that in their antiques business, they must occasionally buy large and expensive pieces of furniture and be prepared to hold them awhile before they sell.

Encouraging your staff to participate in purchasing decisions in meetings or including them in buying trips is an excellent way to delegate responsibility, reward good service, incorporate different points of view, and foster team spirit.

Setting Prices

Keystoning—the setting of prices by doubling all costs—is one of the most widely used pricing formulas. In this process, you first determine your costs—for example, do you pay for shipping, customs duties, export licenses, or travel? If you do, you would double them, as well as the cost of the items themselves, and arrive at your retail price. Linda Campisano has found that she can make a profit on her hats by figuring one third for labor, one third for materials, and one third for overhead, then doubling that wholesale cost to arrive at a retail price, which includes boxes, ribbons, labels, and bags. Another way to look at her calculations is to say that she multiplies her cost of materials, which is easy to measure, by six.

Sellers of expensive items such as valuable jewelry and designer clothing usually set prices higher than keystoning. Elyssa Silbert, who combines rare and colorful gemstones to make jewelry, understands that keystoning the costs of raw materials wouldn't adequately value her taste, training, and knowledge, not to mention her time and energy. She also knows that her customers don't expect low prices for such luxurious goods.

To take account of the perishable nature of their product, florists commonly triple their flower costs. Jen Stone of StoneKelly says, "The first mark-up is for the flowers; the second is for rent, labor, and the container; and the last third is my profit."

Linda Getchell factors her textile expertise into the prices she charges for vintage and antique panels. On one-of-a-kind items like those she has collected at auctions over the years, she definitely feels free to go beyond traditional pricing formulas. At Kate's Paperie, Kate Flax knows she can do more than keystone an item for her three Manhattan paper-plus stores "if we bought it in Italy and it's exotic and exclusive." On the other hand, she'll charge less for something if she bought it at a good price.

At Henry's General Store, Maura Koutoujian begins setting prices by doubling costs, then changes them depending on how she answers subjective questions such as: Was the item difficult to find? Did it take a lot to get it? What would I pay for it? Here, a collection of old-fashioned letter seals is certainly well priced for today's market.

It's crucial to understand what the market will bear for your products and in your specific location or general area. Shirley Maiden knows she can't charge New York City prices for the vintage clothing she sells in Manchester, Vermont. In Manhattan, on the other hand, Pamela Scurry realizes that her Wicker Garden customers aren't coming to her Madison

Just Ask.....
We can special order any style letter available and have it shipped to you!
"Egyptienne" $36.00 per letter
"Elzevir" $25.00 per letter
"Augustea" $26.00 per letter
"Renaissance" $26.00 per letter

Avenue location looking for a bargain, although she tries to have "good value as well as good quality."

Sometimes prices simply can't go as high as you might like. Rhonda Eleish and Edie van Breems are always attending auctions and browsing at other stores so they know exactly what their furniture and accessories should sell for; their prices are never higher than elsewhere, and they might occasionally be lower in order to turn inventory more quickly. This knowledge also leads them to take smaller markups on extremely rare pieces of furniture that "would

QUICK TIPS

What the Market Will Bear

1. What did the item cost you? What did it cost to get it to your shop?
2. Do you bring any special expertise to this product—can you tell a customer how it was made, how to care for it, where to buy it, where to resell it if necessary? You can charge for these "value added" services, especially if they're obvious from the way the item is labeled in the store.
3. How rare is the item? Can it be replaced?
4. What would you spend for it in a shop?
5. If the piece is expensive but you want it to fill a hole in your assortment, how small are you willing to make the markup?
6. What will be the prevailing value in your market, in your town—for this item?
7. Does it have a shelf life?

become exorbitant if we priced them the way we usually do other items." When Ina Garten of Barefoot Contessa realized that the price for the "perfect" brownie would be more than even the eastern Long Island market would bear, she made a slight change in ingredients so she could charge $1.50 instead of $2.00. She now sells her close-to-perfection confections at the rate of 1,000 a week. At French General, when the owners sell more than twelve of any of their Manhattan shop's stock of mostly vintage items to one customer, they call it a wholesale transaction and reduce the price.

Occasional price reductions improve cash flow, bring in shoppers in the off-season, and provide a new reason for owners to communicate with customers. The only problem is that shoppers sometimes begin to expect these discounts and are therefore less willing to buy at full price.

The range of prices available in a shop is another important consideration. Elizabeth Lamont at Room with a View, Lori Hedtler at Devonia, and Linda Getchell, and Rhonda Eleish and Edie van Breems, at their eponymous shops, all discovered that a shop full of Tiffany-priced merchandise rarely succeeds unless your wares are sold in turquoise boxes on Fifth Avenue. Elizabeth, Linda, and Rhonda and Edie broadened their price points by adding gifts to the antiques and home furnishings they originally stocked, while Lori added lines of casual, contemporary dishes and reproduction furniture to her vintage and antique tableware.

Merchandising and Display

A store with appealing merchandise that is well displayed will bring in new shoppers, bring back established shoppers, and keep both groups curious about your stock until they find at least one item to purchase. The way your wares are arranged isn't the only way to get potential customers to linger; shoppers are also drawn to a friendly environment, good conversation, pleasant music, enticing aromas, and a warm welcome. Good display, however, is a good beginning.

A pleasing look is fullness without overcrowding. You don't want so many of any one item that your boutique resembles a discount store, or so few that you seem to be doubting an item's appeal. By arranging your wares in real-life simulations, or vignettes, your shop will look rich in merchandise without actually having large numbers of any one item. At Ta Da! Rosie Daykin sells only three styles of old-fashioned girls' dresses. However, she hangs them in a children's-size closet next to other pieces of children's furniture so the display doesn't look sparse. At Henry's General Store, Maura Koutoujian groups all the bath items in a small space, just as they would be in a home. Nell Hill's Mary Carol Garrity wants to give prominence to the pewter trays, ceramic shells, and glass candleholders she carries. So she displays them in varied, often layered, arrangements on tables, chests, or shelves. Interesting and unexpected display pieces can also make merchandise more appealing. Diane Loesch-Jones of London Lace has turned her ceiling into a display fixture with diaphanous curtains floating overhead.

Mail-Order Success

Unlike many women shop owners for whom stress is a constant companion, Diane Loesch-Jones can honestly say that her professional life is calm. Even on days when no one walks through the door of London Lace, her vintage textile and curtain shop in Boston, her business is profitable. That's because her mail-order business of the same name sends out 1,000 pairs of curtains a month. "Curtains," she explains, "are a perfect catalog item. They don't break, and everyone has more than one window."

Diane first came up with the idea of selling the lace curtains through a catalog to help pay some additional expenses. Her initial attempt, featuring black-and-white photographs of eight sets of curtains, was photocopied at the local copy shop; the only luxurious touch was a high-quality ribbon that held the pages together.

Today, London Lace's "Window Solutions" is a glossy 28-page color booklet filled with window vignettes and descriptions of the curtains, as well as notes about the company, such as its customizing service (which increased business dramatically when it began in 1999). Although the styles are timeless, Diane prints only an eighteen-month supply of catalogs—25,000 copies. This gives her the opportunity to add new patterns and sizes and discontinue unpopular styles. She communicates other news, including price reductions on slow-moving items and factory seconds, via a shopping web site.

Her success with mail order gives Diane the luxury of knowing she could close her doors on expensive Newbury Street at any time and still have a thriving business. But that's unlikely—the mail-order business needs space, the store is self-supporting, and she loves "the very pleasant place to be" that is her shop.

2
Anne Fontaine
PARIS

At Toronto's Putti, the cash wrap is both pretty and practical. Located in the bath area, which replicates a French apothecary, the mahogany counter is backed by floor-to-ceiling shelves. Because someone is always stationed at the counter, a customer who wants a spritz of fragrance, a dollop of hand cream, or a glance at the label of a particular soap can be waited on quickly. This arrangement of product testing provides entertainment for patrons who might otherwise be bored and helps employees keep track of small, easily stolen items.

Anne Fontaine blouse shops throughout the world exemplify the French maxim "One must renounce all but the essential, so the essential may speak." In these stores, where inventory is limited to white and black, fabric and design do the speaking, from organdy to piqué, from tailored to ruffled.

Your shop gets instant and inexpensive freshness when you move the stock around and vary the vignettes. At Nell Hill's, curious customers come to see the changing displays and stay to talk about them with Mary Carol and her friendly staff. At Room with a View, Elizabeth Lamont is forever creating new model rooms so that different tea sets, breakfast dishes, and bedroom and bathroom beautifiers get their moment in the spotlight. She points out that a store with a minimum of interior walls means more flexibility. At Boston's Devonia, change may seem like sleight of hand. Say a customer is interested in pink and green dishes, and the shop's tables are set with blue and gold. While the customer isn't looking, owner Lori Hedtler will surprise her with place settings in the requested colors.

Of course, store decor isn't just about the merchandise; it's also a reflection of the shop owner's personality and style. At Spruce in Manhattan, bright chartreuse walls, visible from the street, immediately convey the attention-getting simplicity and impact favored by owner Gaige Clark. In nearby SoHo, the muted blue walls of French General create a calm atmosphere. It echoes the cozy, friendly way that owners Kaari and Molly Meng like to conduct themselves with customers. Further uptown, Pamela Scurry of Wicker Garden placed a real Victorian porch in

In the nineteenth century, the building housing Henry's General Store was a tavern. The original oak bar used to hold shot glasses and beer steins in the days when Wisconsin was frontier country. Today, it is equally hospitable to the camping supplies and gift items displayed there now.

L'OCCITANE

Signature Packaging

The women who own these shops know that wrapping is much more than a way to get wares home from the store.

At Wild Thyme, Laurie deGrazia wraps flowers in animal-print and gold-striped tissue paper, then puts them in copper-color bags with gold labels. This rich look is her best marketing tool for her society clients in the Philadelphia–Wilmington area.

On New York City's Madison Avenue, Pamela Scurry's Wicker Garden uses tulle instead of tissue paper to make gifts glamorous.

Color is an important aspect of a shop's packaging. At Ta Da!, pale pink boxes are tied with chocolate-brown ribbon bearing the store's name. A sprig of artificial flowers is attached under the bow, and a sticker with the store's logo goes on top of the ribbon. The pink-and-brown sticker is attached to inexpensive generic white shopping bags, too.

The wrappings at White on White in Midland Park, New Jersey, on the other hand, play directly on the store's concept: the freshness of white. Each purchase is tucked into a translucent white sack. A hang tag made from the calling card is attached with an aluminum key chain, and a sprig of lemon leaves is tucked inside.

The basic wrapping at StoneKelly on Manhattan's Upper West Side is natural tissue paper and beautiful ribbon, a sleek backdrop that doesn't compete with the shop's intricate arrangements of flowers. Owner Jen Stone also tries to match the packaging to the recipient (for example, she assumes that a gift giver and a gift recipient have similar taste, and that the parents of a baby named Charlotte would appreciate different wrapping than would the parents of a baby named Ashley).

the middle of her Madison Avenue shop, added green carpet, and created a southern look that graciously sets off the shop's white wicker furniture and accessories. Across the country in Jackson Hole, Wyoming, Cecilia Heffernan got the homey, casual warmth she loves for Flower Hardware by distressing the walls and using old bricks to make a potting shed.

Publicity and Advertising

Word of mouth is a powerful way to bring visitors into your shop. If you want to generate substantial revenue and profits, it helps to do more. Advertising, which costs money, and publicity, which is often free, are excellent vehicles for getting in touch with actual and potential customers and giving them a reason to visit your store.

There is almost total agreement among the women featured in *A Shop of One's Own* that the best way to spend an advertising dollar is to put it into direct mail. When a container filled with antiques arrives, Rhonda Eleish and Edie van Breems share the news through mailings and a notice on their web site. Nina Kaplan's loyal followers—her mailing list numbers five thousand—receive invitations to trunk shows at French Lace in Newtown, Pennsylvania. Using the same list, Nina also "reminds them of my existence" with cards offering a 10 percent discount or a $25 gift certificate.

Parties for holidays, shop openings, and expansions also can pull in people. Carolyn Busch of Fino Fino in Menlo Park, California, started the Peninsula Panama Hat Society as a joke, but the champagne party she holds for it every June draws reporters as well as hat fanciers. Many shops encourage customers to give gifts year-round by creating vignettes that emphasize various holidays and by establishing wedding, baby, and housewarming registries. Books also make fine promotional tools and in-store celebrations. Mary Carol Garrity did very well with *Nell Hill's Style at Home*, Cecilia Heffernan with *Flowers A to Z*, and Ina Garten with her two *Barefoot Contessa* cookbooks.

Printed fabrics are rare at Manhattan's Peacock Alley, a retail label known for textured neutrals of white, stone, ivory, and moss. The name assures customers looking for anything from boudoir pillows to bathrobes that they have found luxury European-style linens made to owner Mary Ella Gabler's demanding specifications.

Promoting Good Deeds

Before she opened Through the Looking Glass in Atlanta, Trina Summins knew she wanted to do more than sell high-end French children's clothing. So she found a way to promote her shop and give back to her community at the same time.

First she created a birthday club, in which her young customers are treated to a day of discount shopping in the month of their birthday. Each boy and girl also receives a birthday gift—

harmonicas and story books are popular. Then Trina makes a donation in the child's name to the Atlanta Children's Shelter, which provides day care for young children so their parents can look for work.

Trina also donates a percentage of the revenues from the store's semi-annual sales to the shelter and sends them clothing in response to specific requests. She hopes that along with a taste for fine French fashions, her young customers will develop a life-long commitment to helping the less fortunate in their community.

Education is another way to entice shoppers. The McCharles House offers well-attended seminars on tea, herbs, and family traditions. Lisa Wofford gives so many classes in so many different crafts, she almost has a whole school operating out of her South Carolina shop, Out of Hand. Kate Flax draws people with demonstrations of gift wrapping and papermaking. To boost attendance, she puts attractive promotional flyers on the cash wrap, places them in every bag, and mails them to her best customers.

There are several ways to use newsletters to communicate with customers. Carolyn Busch sends *Hat Chat*, which includes articles on "How to Build a Hat Wardrobe," "How to Care for Your Hats," and "What Hand Blocking Really Means," to her mailing list of two thousand hat purchasers. The McCharles House, with a list of fifty thousand names—from in-person and Internet guest books—has stopped sending recipes and articles on family traditions, gardening, and architecture through the mail; instead they publish *The McCharles House* on the Internet.

Thank-you notes are hardly a new idea. But in today's world, a graceful note is such a delightful surprise that it can become an effective way to personalize relationships with customers. At the same time, a note is an opportunity to "romance sales" by complimenting shoppers on the "perfection" of their purchases. Linda Campisano spends time trimming stationery with miniature pearls and flowers because her thank-you notes are "more useful than any advertising." Perhaps the best free advertising and surefire way to help customers remember your shop—and to get others to think of you as well—is with distinctive, recyclable shopping bags, such as Eileen Fisher's strong white shoulder totes.

Visitors to Grandmother's Buttons in St. Francisville, Louisiana, can learn the history of buttons at the nearby Button Museum established by owner Susan Davis. The store's exquisite wrapping includes a damask-inspired card, lush ribbon, and its very own button—all too beautiful to throw away.

Most of the shop owners on these pages spend no money on print or broadcast advertising, choosing instead to work for editorial coverage in local and national newspapers and magazines and appearances on cable TV home shows. "Your ad has to appear a dozen times to even be noticed," says Darcy Creech of Peter Beaton Hat Studio, "and the big Ralph Lauren–type spreads in places like the *New York Times Magazine* that do get noticed are much too expensive at fifty thousand dollars an issue to even consider."

Being free isn't the only advantage of editorial over advertising copy. "An article," says

At Liberty in Vancouver, Wendy Williams-Watt designed labels that are stark, elegant, and mince no words. They fit perfectly with the home decor shop's subdued color scheme of mostly white, gray, black, and silver.

The Art of Retail

When Gale Gand owned Vanilla Bean Bakery in Northfield, Illinois (now under different ownership and called Three Tarts Bakery), she needed a way to put the European-style café on the sensory map of suburban Chicago. Her luscious signature coconut-oatmeal and poppy seed cakes, chocolate pecan pie, and vanilla-infused homemade root beer certainly did the trick. She would take classic, old-fahioned recipes, such as banana cream pie (opposite), deepen the flavors, then add such aesthetic flourishes as a circle of chocolate-dusted whipped cream roses.

To elevate her shop above the competition and make sure its name was remembered, Gale designed a forthright logo. Sporting a chef's toque blanche, the logo was clearly visible on everything Vanilla Bean Bakery sold, from granola to biscotti to ten kinds of bread. She had labels made in several sizes to perfectly complement the variety of package sizes, reinforcing the impression that nothing in the shop was left to chance. Even the tissue that goes into every bag is original. Columns of the shop's logo alternate with columns of homey pictures of layer cake, peasant bread, and steaming soup.

VANILLA
BEAN
BAKERY

Rosie Daykin of TaDa!, "gives you a special kind of validation because people read it differently from the way they look at an ad." She sends press kits to the magazine editors who are likely to run stories featuring the kinds of gifts, children's clothing, and home furnishings she sells. "A phone call to an editor, who is always looking for material, can work like a charm. And remember, you have nothing to lose—don't be intimidated or discouraged if your first effort brings no response."

Since the first Wicker Garden opened in 1976, Pamela Scurry's stores have appeared in hundreds of publications, from *Gourmet*, *Architectural Digest*, and *Victoria* to trade publications such as *Small World* and *Children's Business*. It helps to keep track of editors' publishing schedules and to know how often their section appears. Becoming familiar with their taste and supplying them with possible text as well as photos will also work in your favor.

Charitable donations can bring favorable publicity, especially if they're placed where potential customers will learn about your shop. After her twice-yearly sales, Linda Campisano donates unsold hats to an auction that benefits a breast cancer charity.

If you make the decision to advertise, think carefully about where, when, and how you do it. Eileen Main of Farmhouse places ads for her gift and folk art wares in programs for events she herself likes to attend—the Williamstown Theater Festival, Tanglewood concerts, and the local decorators'

QUICK TIPS

Contents of a Press Kit

1. An information sheet with a history of the shop, a description of the merchandise, and every possible way of getting in touch with you.

2. A list of articles about you and your business, plus good-quality copies—in color if you're aiming for magazine coverage—of the most significant stories. The less work the recipient must do, the better.

3. Decorative items with your logo, such as shopping bags, stickers, and gift cards.

4. Reproducible photos of what is new in your shop that might be appropriate for this particular publication and the specific area covered by the editor to whom you're writing.

5. A handwritten note or personal letter saying you will be calling to see if you can be of any further help. Then do call within a few days.

6. Your business card.

Put it all in an attractive folder—professionally printed, if possible—with your name, your shop's name, and your shop's logo.

showcase. She has found this more effective than using local newspapers or restaurant place mats. Lori Hedtler has drawn customers for Devonia's dishes from advertisements in *Boston's Antiques Guide and Guest Informant*, which is in rooms at expensive hotels. Carolyn Busch has come up with a way to make her ads stand out. A few times a year she places an ad in the local paper featuring a customer wearing a Fino Fino hat. The text gives the customer's name and occupation, and a quote about why he or she likes the hat. "This lets people know you don't have to look like a model to wear one of our creations," Carolyn explains.

San Franciscans and visitors alike are drawn to Fino Fino's large selection of hand-blocked panama hats. Although the shop's hats can cost as much as $5,000, most sell for $425 to $800.

Any method of communicating with actual and potential customers will be most effective if it highlights merchandise that is currently "flying off the shelves" and appears

during peak selling periods.

Always display articles and ads featuring your store *in* your store and on your web site. Make certain your entire staff is familiar with all the items appearing in current and recent ads and on editorial pages.

The Internet

One of the major revelations to emerge at the end of the twentieth century was that the Internet wouldn't do away with shopping in stores. Sitting in front of a screen is no substitute for going to a beautiful store with three-dimensional merchandise and people you can look in the eye.

Nevertheless, potential shoppers do spend time "surfing the Net," and web sites can enhance the sales of brick-and-mortar stores. Many shop owners consider web sites an integral part of their overall advertising and publicity strategy. They're an excellent way to communicate with potential customers and can be much more effective than an ad in the Yellow Pages.

Effective site design can be an art in itself; a site that seems shoddy can do more harm than good. At the very least, it should present, in a clear and easy-to-follow format, basic information about merchandise, hours, location, and contact numbers—phone, fax, e-mail—combined with text and photographs that evoke the shop's atmosphere and introduce the merchandise. Try to make it available on a number of search engines for wide and easy access.

The Nell Hill's web site displays merchandise vignettes and conveys the spirit of the shop with a few phrases such as: "Sophisticated yet unpretentious . . . . Romantic while beautifully practical . . . baskets, pillows, vases and dishware." Fino Fino puts the spotlight on customers by showing enticing photographs of them sporting their panamas at the Peninsula Hat Society's annual party. Grasmere demonstrates its desire to please by saying, "If you would like to come in for a consultation on a custom floral design, please call ahead so we will be able to give you our full attention."

Some sites are quite specific about what a shop offers even if the items can't be purchased online. Barefoot Contessa lists the varieties of coffee available by mail by calling its 800 number. The shop's catering menus, also displayed on the site, can both whet appetites and reduce decision-making time for East Hampton locals who visit the store. Anandamali shows the shop's larger mosaic work, including a $5,000 mural.

Rhonda Eleish credits the Eleish–van Breems web site, which includes a virtual tour of the store, with generating half the store's revenue—even though no sales are made online. (Shoppers must phone or visit the store.) The site, which has been up since the store opened in 1997 and is maintained by the shop's manager, receives twenty-one thousand hits a month, many inspired by a sustained local and national print advertising campaign.

Creating opportunities for shopper interaction on your Internet site can leave a strong impression on a web surfer. At the same time it generates useful information for a store. Most sites have a guest book or mailing list. New York City florist Spruce inspires confidence in its wedding planning with a three-page

QUICK TIP

Online Facts

Although it might seem a handicap for a shop to operate without a web site, more than half of the forty women interviewed for *A Shop of One's Own* in the winter of 2002 didn't have one. Of the eighteen who did, only six were actual shop-on-line or "shopping cart" sites. This is because an attractive web site is expensive and time consuming to establish and maintain. If it is an authentic shopping venue, the time and money required to handle the business it produces could detract from your physical shop.

questionnaire that shows it's on top of every detail. Papyrus stationers has a "Reminder Registry" that alerts registered customers when selected holidays and personal events are about to occur and sends a message about what is available for the occasion. Kate's Paperie, which sells directly from the Internet, entices browsers to complete a short market survey by holding a $50 drawing for respondents each month.

Desana

PAULA AND KAREN GOLDSTEIN

Paula Goldstein began Desana, her appointment-only custom fragrance business, in her Seattle apartment in 1996. When she moved to a store on Newbury Street in Boston two years later, she maintained her highly individualized approach. Every customer who makes a purchase from Desana (the name of a South American tribe) has the luxurious experience of having helped create her own personal fragrance.

Desana's first Boston location was decorated by Paula's mother, an interior designer. It featured soothing sage-green decor and eye-catching windows from which a pair of antique lamps beckoned shoppers to browse inside. For her new shop in Boston's South End, she chose a more modern look.

Paula began working with fragrance as a paid intern at a perfumery while earning a degree in musical theater at the Boston Conservatory of Music. She knew instantly that she had found something she loved and was good at—she modestly acknowledges that she is a "nose," one of the few people in

RAGRANC
AFRICAN VIOLET
ArabianRose
BERGAMOT
Black Coconut
CAPPUCCINO
CASSIS
CHINA LILY
DESANA
CUCUMBER LIME
EARTH
EGYPTIAN JASMINE
EGYPTIAN SANDALWOOD
EgyptianMusk
FIG
FOREST RAIN

the world with the innate ability to recognize and remember many different scents.

Women come to Paula's current shop, in Boston's trendy South End, to participate in a time-honored process of creating their perfect fragrance. Starting with a client's preferences as a guide, Paula or an employee begins mixing scents—"citrusy," "sweet," "floral," "musky." The collaborative process continues until it produces the desired scent. For men shopping for women, 25 percent of her clientele, selecting a scent begins with questions about the woman's favorite flower, a perfume she already wears, or a home or wardrobe color scheme. Custom fragrances

Though Desana is home to more than 150 natural oils from Europe, Asia, and Africa, this quantity is minuscule by fragrance-industry standards. "But what we lack in size, we make up for in personal service," says Paula.

can be made up in a two-ounce spray perfume bottle and a quarter-ounce essential oil, as well as body lotion, shower gel, massage oil, shampoo, conditioner, and shaving gel.

For some people, the process is as enjoyable as the resulting perfume itself. Other customers are more willing to be guided. "Our formulators," says Paula, "must be aware and open so that people feel safe and comfortable expressing themselves. Honesty and tact are basic requirements."

The shop encourages customers to return for an adjustment of their fragrance if they're not completely happy. Desana also restores perfumes to their original scent if they have changed over time.

Although the in-person experience is the heart of what Desana offers, the shop also fills phone orders from repeat clients. Even people who have only read about the process can help create a fragrance over the phone by answering a series of questions. Paula then sends out samples based on the phone interview, and keeps refining them until the customer is satisfied.

Many of Desana's clients are women who are allergic to the alcohol and chemicals present in most commercial fragrances. Paula recalls with great pleasure a seventy-year-old woman who told her with tears in her eyes that because of Desana she was able to wear perfume for the first time in her life.

Paula also sells potpourri, candles, and soaps, along with vintage vanity accessories and preblended fragrances. Everything in the store—including the shopping experience itself—is designed to make customers feel pampered and special for at least some part of their busy day.

DESANA

Finding Your Niche

Spruce

Gaige Clark

Spruce stands out. Its rich chartreuse walls are startling even in New York's unconventional Greenwich Village, drawing people into what turns out to be a beautiful oasis in a hectic city. Evergreen shrubs in big green planters on the sidewalk announce that this is a shop that wants to temper the concrete and steel of the city with the bounty of nature.

Gaige Clark found the shop through a tiny classified ad. "I'd been a consultant to a major floral designer but knew I was ready for my own business," she says. After a renovation, the store was born. Its style is what Gaige calls New England garden, a fresh, tailored natural look she pioneered. Most arrangements are monochromatic—three flower varieties in a single strong color balanced by a touch of

Spruce's bounteous flowers spill onto the Manhattan sidewalk, only a few steps away from a busy three-street intersection. To attract the notice of passersby, flowers are unwrapped, cut, and arranged on tables just inside the windows.

Spruce

green—and look as if they're growing out of their containers of terra-cotta, wood, or clear glass.

After seeing what sold best in past years, Gaige eliminated candles, soaps, and garden products to concentrate fully on flowers and plants. Believing the dictum that "less is more," she chooses a few unusual plants each season and buys them in enough volume to make a statement. Around Christmas, Spruce's poinsettias aren't the traditional flat-leaved white or red varieties but the rarer Windsor Rose, with ruffled pink petals and curvy, intensely green leaves. They're displayed in identical terra-cotta pots on shelves lining the store, some standing upright and others balanced on their sides with the plants protruding horizontally; a few are even perched on up-ended sturdy birch logs on the floor. In addition, there's a shelf devoted to Christmas cactus and another to baby's tears, a signature variety for the shop.

In this incredibly inviting shop, most of the vibrantly colored flowers are out in clear glass containers on distressed metal tables; only a few are kept in the almost hidden refrigerator case in the back. And yes, the shop is kept quite cold to prolong the life of the flowers.

Containers, from rustic wood boxes to simple glass, are chosen so they won't compete with the blossoms they hold. The shop is partial to roses and ranunculus because they are available in so many strong colors.

Spruce's packaging is all chartreuse and green tissue paper and ribbon to echo the store's elegant minimalism. Attention to visual detail also shows up on the shop's interactive

web site and in a dusty pink four-page brochure of the store's floral designs, which changes twice a year.

Gaige's great-grandmother grew peonies and gladioluses for Henry Ford, so in a sense she's gone back to her roots. Maybe that's why everything at Spruce seems so down-to-earth. That includes employees happily picking up and redoing arrangements, as well as Gaige's straightforward advice to lovelorn men: "Be yourself—and spend $300."

Flowers in containers are encased in a clear tote tied with pretty ribbon (opposite). Business cards and care instructions are printed on white and slate-colored paper (above).

SPRUCE

Peggy Jean's Pies

PEGGY DAY AND JEANNE WAGSTER

At Peggy Jean's Pies in Columbia, Missouri, Peggy Day and Jeanne Wagster do everything with care. In 1993, before they opened their first shop, they took a random phone survey of one hundred people in their area. They call it a "little survey," but it had four pages of every possible question about pies. That survey turned out to be their first high-quality product.

Peggy Jean's beautiful new shop—its third since the partners started the business—is at once homey and grand. With a red brick exterior, floor-to-ceiling windows, and spacious interior, it's large enough to house both the bakery and a thriving luncheonette.

When people kept *them* on the phone because they missed homemade pies so much, and when everyone—men in particular—wanted to talk about their mother's pies, Peggy and Jean knew they had found their escape route out of the world of banking. They also realized that with "Mom's apple pie"—real or imagined—as their main competition, their

PEGGY • JEAN'S
PIES

pies had to be extremely good in order for them to succeed.

The women rented a 700-square-foot shop in the back of a used-car lot and behind a store selling guns and bait, bought a home oven (it was all they could afford), and started baking. They drove around town giving away their apple pies to restaurants, and pretty soon people started ordering them. In the beginning, Peggy had to stand at the front door and wave her apron to let customers know they were in the right place. But after the local paper gave them a write-up, Columbia residents started coming in droves. They've been eating Peggy Jean's pies ever since.

Lifelong friends, Jeanne and Peggy have never been anything but state-of-the-art when it comes to quality. The recipes are from Peggy's family archives, and some of them are two hundred years old. All the ingredients are fresh and natural, with no preservatives or food colorings. The chocolate in the meringue pies is Hershey's cocoa because that's what the original recipe specified. They still mix the dough and measure the dry ingredients for the fillings themselves. Employees roll the dough by hand. Then each pie filling—peach praline and chocolate bourbon pecan as well as traditional apple, cherry, and pumpkin—is made one at a time. "We don't like mass-produced food," says Jeanne. "We're adamant about that." Amazingly, in a shop that typically sells 200 pies a week and might do

One of the bakery's most successful innovations is the baby pie, a two-serving niche product. It comes in the same varieties as the full-size pies, sells for $3.95 to $4.25, and has turned out to be a big money maker for the shop.

The luncheon menu now includes soup from Peggy's family recipe, quiche made with the shop's pie crust, and eight different sandwiches. With baking aromas hanging in the air, sunlight streaming through the windows, delicious food, and the owners' genuine warmth and hospitality, the shop has understandably become a favorite with locals.

800 each for Christmas and Thanksgiving, the only special equipment is a commercial refrigerator and a dough mixer.

To get Mom's quality, Peggy and Jeanne not only use Mom's ingredients, they also use Mom-style Pyrex glass dishes (for which clients pay a deposit) instead of throw-away tins. "People said we were ridiculous," explains Jeanne, "but we felt strongly about the glass. It makes a better pie and a better presentation at the table."

Customer service is high quality as well. The shop's motto is "And then some": if someone is unhappy with a pie, she's given a free lunch as well as a replacement pie. Packaging is beautiful as well as functional. Kraft boxes heavy enough to support a pie and plate—seven pounds altogether—are decorated with red-and-white gingham labels and tied with huge red bows. Handwritten thank-you notes and free delivery in the Columbia area are also available. Repeat customers can pay later. "We're trying to go back to the way things were fifty years ago," Jeanne explains.

Although the original shop was a great little place in which to begin, a year later Peggy Jean's Pies moved to a 3,000-square-foot space in downtown Columbia. It was a huge mistake: The partners hadn't realized that their pies would be too expensive for the local foot traffic or that inconvenient parking would keep other customers away. It took seven years to move again. Today the shop is in the most affluent section of town, large enough at 3,500 square feet to accommodate a twenty-one–person staff and a sizable luncheonette.

Peggy and Jeanne often speak at forums for aspiring business people. "If you're ready to have a baby, you're ready to go into business," they tell the audience. "When it's new, it takes all your energy, and even as it grows you can never get away from it. Capital is like baby food, and there are always unexpected expenses."

Jeanne adds, "After eight years our baby is just now getting to kindergarten, which means we have a little bit more free time—but not much."

Mail orders are filled with extra care. The shop prides itself on shipping pies the day they're baked to assure maximum freshness. They're packed in Styrofoam boxes (here a gift package of six baby pies) and tied with a cheery bow.

Graphic Personality

Dancing Deer Baking Co.

TRISH KARTER

he name Dancing Deer may seem an odd one for a bakery. But the delightful image it conjures up is well suited to a company that has won Boston's heart with its delicious gourmet goods. This playful mood is also reflected in the bakery's graphics. Its card features a stick-figure baker, white toque and all, pointing with pride to a tin of cupcakes being taken from the oven. And the deer seems to be dancing for joy. All these whimsical figures have a lot to be proud of: Dancing Deer has won numerous national and regional awards for its all-natural baked items, including intensely flavored chocolate espresso and gingerbread cakes.

To stand out on the crowded shelves of prepackaged desserts, Dancing Deer Baking Co. uses playful graphic images, executed on subtle-colored lightweight cardboard. They communicate instantly that these are extraordinary products.

CEO Trish Karter, whose background includes both finance and art, began her

DANCING DEER CO.
5197 WASHINGTON ST. WEST ROXBURY, MA 02132 tel. 617.469.2021
NCING DEER
BAKING CO.

association with Dancing Deer Baking Co. in the early 1990s when she and her husband became investors. By 1995 the bakery was selling to restaurants and cafés throughout New England, and Trish was working there full time, managing the business aspects of the company. Then Dancing Deer got into the mail-order and wholesale business through sheer accident: A Food and Home Channel producer discovered the bakery when he made a wrong turn on the way to a dinner party, found himself at Dancing Deer, bought some gingerbread cake for his hosts, and decided to put the company on television.

Trish knew she wanted a name and logo that would express the company's life-loving personality, its pure flavors, its naturalness, and its business ethic. The look she had in mind would be clever yet unpretentious. She got all her wishes. The rendering of the sprightly dancing deer joyfully conveys a connection with nature, a unique aesthetic, and an enthusiasm for the product. The words "yummy," "tasty," "nibble," and "chew" are printed all over the boxes and bags; cardboard inserts supply lists of ingredients and ideas on how to serve each product. Trish points out that Dancing Deer's packaging is not only appealing but honest: "Our cookie package," she says, "looks like others, but because it's not filled with air it weighs twice as much. We

Multihued frosting and saw-tooth edges on Dancing Deer's popular lavender-flavored shortbread cookies are a new twist on this old favorite, but the fresh butter is true to its Scottish origins. Other innovative cookie flavors are chocolate tangerine, sugar cane lime, and peanut butter honey.

get continual feedback that our originality is paying off."

To get the right graphics for the company, Trish called on a former colleague, Susan Slover, a top New York graphic artist whose client list included Bergdorf Goodman, Coach, and Gucci. At first Trish was hesitant to approach Susan because she knew that her company's fees were beyond the fledgling company's reach. But in 1995, when Trish finally told Susan about her ideas, Susan insisted on being involved in the enterprise. She's now a shareholder, and her design ideas are a crucial part of the company's image.

Dancing Deer has a strong commitment to its employees and to the working-class Roxbury community where it began. It provides health, disability, life, and bereavement insurance, rewards overtime, and gives all employees stock at par value. When it needed more space, it made a point of finding a new location that would be accessible by bus to its staff. To aid the community, it produces a special house-shaped cookie and donates all proceeds from its sale to Sweet Homes, a local project to end homelessness.

Pansies sculpted from white chocolate adorn a special-order buttermilk cake with wild blueberry filling. The goal at Dancing Deer is to "delight the eye and the palate and to have fun at it everyday." This message goes into each package, along with instructions on how to keep the all-natural, no-preservative cakes and cookies fresh, and information on other Dancing Deer products.

DANCING
DEER
BAKING CO.
molasses
clove
cookies

The cellophane-wrapped molasses clove cookie ("soft and homey," says the online catalog) has won the food industry's equivalent of the Oscar. Another perennial favorite is the frosted chocolate espresso cake, even better when served with a scoop of cappuccino ice cream and a drizzle of fresh berry coulis.

RELATING TO PEOPLE

Personal goals and lifestyle preferences will have a strong influence on business decisions once your shop is up and running. Will you hire a staff so you can pull back from sixteen-hour days? Will you expand into more shops or carry different merchandise? What is the definition of success, anyway? For Starbucks, it's more than four thousand stores around the world. You may have a different dream.

Judy Green's GARDEN

Building a Staff

Before you start hiring people on a permanent basis, ask yourself an important, if obvious, question: Do you really need paid employees? A frank evaluation of your shop's operations may show that helping customers, keeping records, and stocking and arranging wares aren't getting done in a timely fashion. Could you solve the problem by shortening your store hours and using that time for financial or inventory management? Perhaps your shop is busy only five days a week. Or you might be able to take advantage of the tradition that allows certain kinds of shops such as art galleries and antiques shops to have short and erratic, though clearly posted, hours. Maybe part-time or temporary employees would be a less expensive way to solve your staffing problems than full-time, year-round help.

Rather than hiring people to take over, you might also consider closing when you're away on trips. Rosie Daykin shuts her doors at Ta Da! when she goes on Paris buying trips; she's greeted on her return by customers eager to see her purchases. Lisa Wofford reduces staff requirements at her Out of Hand shop in Mount Pleasant, South Carolina, by placing her desk on the selling floor so she can talk to customers and work on the computer efficiently.

Along with top-of-the-line garden tools, plants, and furnishings at Judy Green's Garden Shop in London, owner Judy Green offers lectures and classes in container gardening. She can also turn consultant and whip a garden into glorious shape.

Running a shop can mean nonstop socializing. Only you can determine if you're likely to thrive in that environment or if additional help in the store could prevent a burnout resulting from never taking a break.

If you do decide to hire someone, ask yourself some hard questions before you begin your search. How much responsibility do you want to delegate and how much authority are you willing to give away? If you think you need someone who can do everything you do, be aware that a high-powered person may not take direction easily. It might be wiser to choose someone who compensates for your weaknesses rather than duplicating your strengths. If, for example, you don't enjoy keeping records, having a bookkeeper or an accountant a few hours a week or a few days a month would be an excellent solution.

Laurie deGrazia of Wild Thyme near Wilmington, Delaware, came to the conclusion that instead of hiring designers, it was better to look for people who had no training in design but lots of innate talent. "They work more quickly, I can pay them less, and they'll follow the specified design rather than inventing one of their own."

Word of mouth—through family, friends, or current employees or customers—is one of the most reliable and successful methods for finding employees. A HELP WANTED sign in the shop's window has a good chance of attracting people who will relate well to your customers; they may even *be* your customers. Contacting local colleges and putting ads in the local papers and on the Internet are also good ways of finding potential candidates.

LESSONS
Working with Employees

At Wild Thyme florist outside Wilmington, Delaware, Laurie deGrazia has learned that everyone she hires doesn't have to be creative. The shop needs people to deliver as well as design flowers, to do the accounts and unpack boxes, and to be good with customers. She looks for talented but untrained people because it is more economical for the store in the long run.

Rosie Daykin at Ta Da! in Vancouver wants to hire women for her gift and children's boutique who aren't interested in opening their own stores. She wants a woman to see working with her as something that's fun, "a bit of a treat she is giving herself."

Linda Campisano has learned that her notion that people would flourish if she just treated them well was wrong. She now does two or three interviews per person before hiring someone for her millinery shops. She also knows that if she does everything herself, her employees don't get to find out what they're capable of. "You aren't as needed as you think you are, once you let people do their jobs," she says.

Vivian Heredia of The McCharles House tries to reduce turnover by giving directions to her bilingual staff in both Spanish and English. Her "training and retraining" takes the form of staff meetings once or twice a week, at which she discusses topics such as greeting people and what is going on in the world that might be on customers' minds.

Nest Feathers' Neva Scott points out to new employees that there are no signs in the store saying "no" to anything. "I tell them we say yes, yes, yes to customers, and that's what I want them to do."

Putti

You can buy a standard job application form at any office supply store, but interviews are intensely personal interactions and can take many shapes. Laurie deGrazia asks applicants to duplicate her most popular floral designs, then hires those who accomplish the task accurately and quickly. Beth Siqueland-Gresch stresses the hard work and tough conditions that exist beyond Grasmere's lovely selling floor, such as hauling dirt and containers in 20-degree weather for a Christmas deadline. Trish Karter at Dancing Deer bakery also believes strongly in full disclosure: She lets applicants know hers is

Customer service is a global affair at Putti Fine Furnishings in Toronto. If a shopper can't find vintage linens with her own monogram, the store will do a search for her, as far as away France if necessary.

an entrepreneurial business that is "resource short, pushing hard, doing something new every day, chaotic, and definitely not for the fainthearted. If that description doesn't scare them off, they're hired." Because her stores are located in small-town Atchison, Kansas, miles from any city, Mary Carol Garrity knows many of her employees as neighbors and friends before she hires them.

Start each hire with a trial period during which you can part ways relatively easily if things aren't working out. With a

QUICK TIP

Body Language

In a small shop, everyone interacts with customers, whether selling is their primary responsibility or not. You should feel confident that every one of your employees understands how to read a shopper's needs—when to step in to help, when to back off and let a customer browse.

formal hiring commitment, terminating a relationship may require written warnings and personnel file documentation, to protect against possible claims of unlawful discrimination. Review the employee's performance with her at least once during the trial period so she understands exactly what is expected of her and where she might need to improve.

Training

A thorough training program includes oral instruction from the shop owner or manager, a chance for the new employee to observe the shop during business hours, and written instructions about the more technical aspects of the business. Printed information on sales and returns procedures; store policies regarding credit cards, checks, returns, food, and pets; special services for customers, as well as benefits for employees, should be available for study off the job.

Your policies with regard to employee behavior should also be spelled out in writing. Michéle Rosier of Flowers by Michéle in Santa Monica, California, has employees sign a document that states that they understand they will be terminated if they are caught shoplifting even once. You might add use of alcohol or drugs on the job to a list of absolute prohibitions.

Because it is a nationwide organization, Papyrus needs uniform training procedures to ensure consistent experiences in its one hundred forty fine-paper stores. Before new recruits learn operational details, they spend a full day hearing about the softer side of the business, such as the products offered and the service standard, which always puts the customer first. After that there are videos, guidelines, tips, even testing and role playing so employees understand the consumer's point of view. To ensure that all merchandise display and window designs meet the Papyrus specifications, stores send photographs to district offices and receive an instructional visit if the pictures don't meet company standards.

At Flowers by Cecilia and Flower Hardware in Jackson Hole, Wyoming, Cecilia Heffernan uses her own book, *flowers A to Z,* to train her staff in every aspect of flower beauty and care.

Although the word "training" sounds like an effort aimed only at new people, it should be a continual process that includes everyone. Through weekly or biweekly staff meetings you can give information about new products and policies, helpful advice, constant reinforcement, and meaningful praise for improvement or a job well done. All will help an operation run smoothly.

DELEGATING

Giving the people you've hired responsibility for specific aspects of work in your shop is the very reason you hired them in the first place. There are many compelling reasons to delegate responsibility: You can't or don't want to do something yourself; there are other things you have to do at that particular time; someone else can do it as well as or better than you; it will make the other person feel good—about herself, about the shop, and about you.

Nina Kaplan, who sells clothing, jewelry, and vintage treasures of all kinds at French Lace and Angel Heart in Newtown, Pennsylvania, lets her store managers, who have been with her for years, "really manage." They supervise the other employees, schedule the work week, and even do some buying, which keeps them involved in the creative part of the enterprise. At Eleish–van Breems Antiques, the owners make it a point to have employees observe their selling style before they are given the freedom to sell on their own.

For some women, delegating comes naturally; for others it's a struggle. Rosie Daykin finds it hard to let go of her own vision, but she's learning to "let people do the job I've hired them for because

QUICK TIP

Sharing Your Success

Workers at Dancing Deer Baking Co. in Boston have lots of benefits, including a stock ownership plan, but owner Trish Karter believes what keeps a person in a job isn't money but respect. "We let them see that we believe that good ideas can come from anywhere in the company," she says. "We sit down and open our books with the staff, even though we're a privately held company and don't have to." She tries to educate the staff about how the company works and what makes it profitable. And then she pushes people to use all their capabilities—which sometimes means pushing them to jobs outside Dancing Deer.

in the end it frees me up to do more of the creative work I love." Linda Campisano echoes her thoughts: "If I do everything, my employees won't get to do what they can do, which holds them back and holds me back, too." Be crystal clear about what the job entails and how much responsibility goes along with it. Do you expect the

person to work unsupervised? If so, who will decide if a good job is being done? If there is supervision, who is responsible for it? Have you created an atmosphere with enough freedom so that everyone knows she can ask questions and ask for help? Can everyone trust you, as the final word in any disagreement, to be impartial among all the members of your staff?

Going beyond delegation to participation —the most successful way to operate an enterprise—happens when owners are open about all aspects of the business, encourage employees to be creative, and acknowledge their contributions. Rhonda Eleish says that her

Because they feel so appreciated, and because they care for and love the merchandise, employees at French Lace and Angel Heart in Newtown, Pennsylvania, make a huge contribution to the shops' inviting atmosphere.

shop is so collegial that it feels as if the partnership extends beyond the business arrangement between her and Edie van Breems. Trish Karter fosters an environment in which everyone gets respect, every job is important, and any idea, no matter its origin, is taken seriously.

You may want to turn collegial feelings into tangible rewards. You can institute a profit-sharing program—an incentive program in which a company pays out a percentage of its profits to employees—or offer a partnership arrangement to your most valuable employees.

Problem Solving

If your shop is beset by tension or dissatisfaction, examining and acknowledging what your own role might be is a good first step toward improving the situation. If you've been overly controlling, unclear about duties, playing favorites, making promises you can't fulfill, or withholding praise for a job well done, your behavior needs to be changed first.

Mary Carol Garrity's tip for trying to avoid trouble with her fifty-plus workforce at Nell Hill's is to let each person know that coming to her should be the first step in trying to rectify a difficult situation. "With that many people," Mary Carol says, "there's always the possibility of bad chemistry. If an employee has a bad attitude or I don't like something, I address it immediately."

Community Spirit

It's not surprising that a community feeling prevails at Henry's General Store, located in the lakefront resort town of Princeton, Wisconsin. The shop is in an 1884 tavern that had been in the same family since 1898; current owner Maura Koutoujian bought it from a descendant of that family. Over the years it has evolved into the General Store, selling a whimsical mix of cards, toys, bath accessories, gourmet foods, canoes, and outerwear, plus Maura's favorite wines and cookbooks. Maura adds one unique, classic item—she calls them "quintessences"—to her stock each season; these have included sterling silver baby spoons in the shape of an airplane, black pottery dishes and cookware from Colombia, and standing cast-iron cows that can serve as doorstops or bookends. These eccentric, special pieces are virtual magnets for shoppers, some of whom travel more than three hours to check out each year's new selection.

The shop's true spirit shows up as camaraderie among local merchants, who keep an eye on neighbors' stores and children, make it a point not to stock overlapping merchandise, and freely suggest new items to each other. People of all ages feel comfortable in Henry's, where all receipts are written by hand, and a wooden till with finger codes is still in use. (A computer is used for record keeping.) Maura gets coffee for customers, which is "a little more personal than just leaving it out."

Maura began involving the community when she participated in the Heartland AIDS Bike Ride—five hundred miles in five and a half days—and offered Henry's T-shirts to anyone who sponsored her for $250 or more. She also had travel mugs made up with the Henry's logo. She now donates a percentage of the revenues from the shirt and mug to support a participant in the annual ride.

EXPANSION

One of the most appealing aspects of having a shop is the opportunity to live a life filled with variety. Merchandise, decor, and the people with whom you interact change daily, seasonally, and as the years go on. Many women in *A Shop of One's Own* find

QUICK TIPS

Growing Smart

Eileen Fisher, with twenty-five women's clothing stores throughout the United States, offers the following advice on expanding a business:

1. **Have a unique, expandable idea.**
2. **Know your customer.**
3. **Use mistakes as opportunities.**
4. **Think small. Even as your business grows, maintain a sense of it as a small company.**
5. **Be creative.**
6. **Grow naturally. Don't force things.**

this type of fluctuation totally fulfilling; others have chosen to change the shape of their operation by opening additional stores, selling what they make wholesale, expanding into mail-order sales, or scaling back.

Cecilia Heffernan's path has always been filled with flowers, but it has taken several unpredictable, though always pleasant, turns.

In 1992 she left the life of a ski bum to open a 200-square-foot flower store in Jackson Hole, Wyoming. Three years later she closed the retail, or cash and carry, part of her business to concentrate on custom floral designs. At that point she wanted to stay small. But when customers began asking for advice on gardens and interiors, she found that she loved this personal aspect of design even more than she loved doing flower arrangements for parties. In 2000, with two big factors in her favor—she knew exactly what she wanted to accomplish, and she already had a secure customer base—Cecilia opened Flower Hardware, which sells indoor and outdoor decorative objects, gardening tools, flower and plant containers, and even cash-and-carry flowers. She says her decisions have always been governed by doing what she loves; she has made major changes carefully and deliberately, always making sure a good staff was in place to take over the work she was leaving.

Paula Goldstein of Desana moved into two new things at once—wholesaling her fragrances and a new Boston location for her retail shop. She was prepared to succeed at both because she had done the homework that enabled her to make reasonably accurate projections of costs and revenues in both endeavors, and she took pains to make sure that the second business wouldn't weigh down the first.

Other women learned the hard way about some pitfalls of expanding. Linda Campisano warns that an investor who might make expansion possible may want too much control and divert you from what you love and can sell. Pamela Scurry, who has gone from one store to three and now is back to one, also offers a financial caveat: "Don't let your ego obscure your view of the bottom line. More revenues can actually lead to less in the way of profits." Lisa Wofford, who struggled with the decision of whether to run one store or two, warns that it's a lot easier to branch out if your operation is streamlined. "Keep it simple," she says, "or it gets overwhelming."

Pamela Scurry first brought her white wicker furniture to Manhattan in 1977 with Wicker Garden, then added Wicker Baby and Children shops. By 2001, she was back to one store, and expanded into licensing with her Cottage Garden Collection and French Country Collection.

Pamela Scurry's
Wicker Garden

Jo Malone
London
Amber &
Lavender
Bath Oil
Jo Malone
London

Linda Campisano had learned enough so that when she opened a second millinery store in downtown Chicago, she did it on a shoestring; her expenses barely went beyond the very reasonable rent. For decor she let her hats and her hat blocks (and her expertise in using them) speak for themselves, and as she had hoped, customers were drawn in by curiosity about how hats are actually created. She also knew to leave the first store in the care of her capable manager, in order to become a strong presence at the new location.

The timing must also be right in terms of other aspects of your life. When she was expecting her third child, Eileen Main made the decision to close Farmhouse in downtown Bennington, Vermont, and sell the same gifts, crafts, and artists' work on the Internet and from her barn at open houses several weekends a year. "I don't want to be emptying boxes when I should be making a casserole or cupcakes," she says. "There's not enough of me. I know I'll miss my shop, but my kids will only be young for a little while, and I plan to open again in ten years. This is a pause, not a finale."

The attention, energy, enthusiasm, experience, and capital that make a shop owner successful are the very same qualities that will make an expansion succeed.

Jo Malone was one of the most sought-after facialists in London when she began making soaps, scents, and sprays to sell through her mail-order business, Send a Scent. In 1994 she opened a small shop in London, followed by two more. In 2000 she became part of the Estée Lauder empire and now has a shop and department store boutique in Manhattan.

Hard-Won Lessons

Michéle Rosier thought becoming a business success would be easy: She would just have to be cute and lovable. She had experience being both, from the days when her mother dressed her in *Little House on the Prairie* costumes and sold flowers from a rickshaw cart. And as a member of a professional ice-skating tour for five years, she had collected some business experience. But when she decided to open a flower shop at the age of twenty-three, she found she had a lot to learn.

Location was her first learning experience. Despite its glamorous cachet, Beverly Hills was filled with conservative, price-conscious, demanding people—people who weren't the ideal customers for her high-end shop. Surprisingly, having a busy drugstore across the street didn't necessarily mean lots of traffic for her business. With hindsight, she now sees the value of working at a location before committing to opening your own business there.

Michéle was also startled to learn that rent was just the beginning of her costs. There were separate bills for "triple net"—payments to building managers, gardeners, and window cleaners, allocated among tenants and varying from month to month—as well as taxes and insurance.

Dealing with credit was another hard-won lesson as she accumulated several years' worth of expensive debt on credit cards when her savings ran out before her shop was established.

But expanding too fast taught Michéle her most painful lesson. With the store in Beverly Hills in full swing, she opened a branch in Burbank, then joined an elite group of merchants operating under the aegis of Fred Segal in Santa Monica. With three locations, Michéle says she was "going crazy, heading for a mental breakdown at the age of thirty." When a survey of her five hundred regular customers and her employees told her she would do fine if she limited her selling space to Santa Monica, she closed the doors to the Beverly Hills and Burbank shops and enjoyed "the happiest day of my life." She adds, "By that time my customers trusted me, so they didn't have to see the shop. A successful florist can work out of a warehouse." She encourages this loyalty by not charging for delivery.

Michéle has never had a problem arranging flowers. But it turns out that flowers are about more than beauty, and Michéle now knows about growers, heat waves, and 1:00 A.M. phone calls to her European suppliers. She took a four-month, five-day-a-week course in the mechanics of flower arranging, to complement her natural talent and stylishness.

Early on, Michéle made two advertising missteps—*Penny Saver* ads and freebies at her first store launching. Then she realized that in Los Angeles, where everyone is always in a car, her best ad strategy would be her logo on her delivery trucks. She also does celebrity parties, which have given her good magazine credits; this and her clients' word-of-mouth references have brought her lucrative work on many movie sets.

Even with just one location, Michéle sometimes has as many as fifty people working for her on a film or a special event. She has several drivers, a general manager, and an assistant, as well as eight to ten full-time designers. She loves being able to have "a flexible mix of work and leisure and be in a position to do exactly what I want with my life." She has learned her lessons well.

SCALING BACK

The Peter Beaton Hat Studio

DARCY CREECH

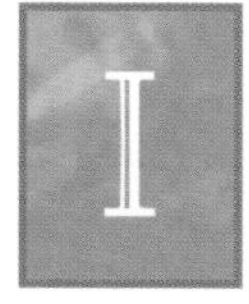

In 1994, after five years accumulating "skills and bills," Darcy Creech sold her line of custom hats to a larger company. As part of that company, she spent a year doing "back flips" for department stores, shipping but not always being paid, and enduring the tremendous pressure of participating in trade shows. This was also a time when she wasn't getting needed advertising or marketing support from the parent company, so it wasn't entirely surprising when her business was jettisoned from the company after a failed IPO.

With money from her buyout, Darcy purchased a 100-year-old building in an area zoned for residential and commercial use, then completely renovated it. One of the reasons she chose Nantucket is that her son, Peter, fell in love with the island on a family vacation.

With two young sons at home, Darcy decided this was the right time to rethink her professional life. Fortified with the buyout of her six-figure contract, and further aided by a couple who support a small number of

THE PETER BEATON HAT ST

BASEBALL
Master Photographers
KITCHENS
LEADING LADIES
CAPE COD & THE ISLANDS
ANSEL ADAMS
NEW YORK
LINDA GOODMAN'S LOVE SIGNS
NEW ENGLAND
BEING DIGITAL
CARE OF THE SOUL
ITALY
FLORENCE & TUSCANY
SIMPLY HALSTON
PARIS ACCESS
THE ANDY WARHOL DIARIES
The Courage to Heal
Casablanca
Bob Woodward
Carl Bernstein
THE FINAL DAYS
BARBARA BUSH
COTTAGES
CUTWATER
FRENCH COUNTRY
JFK
WEDDINGS
JOHN SINGER SARGENT
NEW ENGLAND
KATHARINE
slaves of new york
tama janowitz
FAMILY HOUSES by the SEA

promising entrepreneurs and had helped her in her original business, Darcy decided to relocate her family to Nantucket. In 1995 she found a house in a commercially zoned area that would serve as her home and house her new business. She completely renovated the building, and created a small shop/studio in front.

Since 1996, Darcy has been running her hat studio out of her home. (She named it Peter Beaton Hats for her older son.) She keeps the scope of the business small instead of frantically trying to build a big company. Her hats are crafted in Italy of fine straw and custom trimmed with luxurious ribbon that Darcy designs. All have a classic New England look. Darcy also designs and sells tote bags, ribbon belts, shoes, and sunglasses.

This strategic scaling back doesn't mean that Darcy has stopped thinking about the future. She chose Nantucket not just for its rambling roses and gray weathered shingles, but because it's an international hub filled with style setters who are likely to be noticed for what they are wearing. It's also a favorite of magazine editors, whom Darcy makes sure to contact with pictures and well-timed stories about her newest offerings.

A view from the living room reveals the sun-filled studio where Darcy receives a steady flow of visitors from April through December. Her living quarters are warm with family photos and mellow, childproof pieces. "I love decorating," she says. "A business selling home furnishings is my goal once my sons are bigger."

Though Darcy is generally pleased with the way her business is going—she especially likes the fact that her profit margins aren't shrunk by trade-show or advertising expenses—

she has had trouble locating factories willing to make the small quantities she requires. When she does, they charge her more per item than they do customers with larger orders. One solution to this problem would be to open a second shop, but this is a difficult decision for her. She expanded into another shop, in Palm Beach, Florida, four years after opening her Nantucket studio, but closed it a year later. She is, however, concentrating more on wholesale accounts and making good use of her newly enhanced "shopping cart" web site to communicate with retailers and other customers.

As Darcy contemplates her business's future, she's determined to incorporate the lessons of her past. Before her first company was bought, she had unwisely spent a $75,000 line of credit employing "miracle makers" who promised her enormous sales and multiple media exposure. Now she ties compensation to performance, and she doesn't pay for miracles until they have occurred. She has also learned to be a tough negotiator.

Turn-of-the-century machines made for sewing on straw, like the one Darcy displays in her shop, are still used in the Italian factory where Peter Beaton hats originate. Darcy custom-fits every hat, then helps shoppers choose trim from hundreds of ribbons. The ribbons are easily replaceable, so customers often come back to get a whole new look.

Darcy is moving carefully now, enjoying a less pressured, more balanced life, running a store that is attached to her home and keeping hours that wax and wane with the seasons. At the same time she is beginning to move cautiously back toward a larger operation. Her children's reaction to her career convinces her that she's doing the right thing. On an

application to prep school, her older son wrote that he remembers eating rice and beans when he was three and his mother was struggling, and that now he is proud of her success. In fact, he considers her a role model for his life.

"These hats are as perfect with a linen sheath as they are with jeans," says Darcy. "Their timeless shapes work anywhere." Hillary Rodham Clinton selected a Darcy Creech creation to wear to her husband's inauguration in 1993.

PETER BEATON
PETER BEATON
PETER BEATON

Red Carpet Service

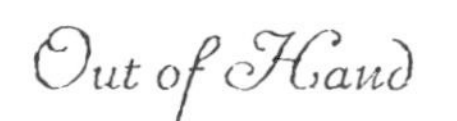

Lisa Wofford

When Lisa Wofford talks about herself and her stores in Beaufort and Mount Pleasant, South Carolina, she says she wants to be a good neighbor and a good friend. She succeeds at both, beginning with her employees. The people she hires for her antiques, gift, and crafts boutiques must "embrace the chaos" of working in what she calls "the middle of life." The phone may be ringing, a UPS man is delivering fifty boxes. At the same time, one customer wants help in choosing among scarves, handbags, and jewelry for a special gift, another is trying to decide between an antique table and one with a more funky look, and a third is buying flowers for a dinner party. Meanwhile, the shoppers'

Out of Hand is housed in a schoolhouse built in the 1860s for free blacks. Today, this gift and crafts shop is something of a school again. Customers can find the best materials available to make everything from invitations to jewelry to lamp shades, as well as expert classes on how to do it.

915
The Art Of Creating

KIT
VOTIVO

children and Lisa's three-year-old daughter play at chalkboard tables in the rear of the store. If applicants are able to take this activity in stride, they're hired.

Lisa trains her staff, gives them responsibility in the area in which they're naturally strong—whether it's flowers, antiques, housewares, or display—and encourages them to grow. One employee, who has been with Lisa since she opened the Beaufort shop in 1996, is a jewelry designer whose creations are now sold in the shop. Employees truly feel at home in the one-room, wood-frame schoolhouse that became the Beaufort shop, and the old red-brick building that Lisa took over in Mt. Pleasant. They even stop by on their days off.

Lisa also treats customers with care. Both Beaufort and Mount Pleasant, outside Charleston, are beautiful antebellum towns attracting tourists and movie crews. But Out of Hand really rolls out the red carpet for local shoppers, whose loyalty is earned and repaid with crafts classes, special orders, and flowers for weddings and other events. Lisa never says no to customers' requests—including holding a child's birthday party in the store. Advice on weddings and decorating comes free of charge.

In the stationery section, colored papers, handmade books, vintage postcards, and fine inks and pens are arranged to start ideas flowing. Lisa believes in creating the perfect ambience to get people to explore their own creativity.

Good customers receive thank-you notes, and sometimes cards and flowers, on both happy and sad occasions. Lisa calls this

"relationship marketing," which she learned in business courses and from observing members of her family who interact well with people. Lisa also remembers being made to feel bad as a child in stores because she didn't have much money to spend, so she treats all customers the same, regardless of how much they want to spend.

On Thursday evenings, students come to Out of Hand to learn how to make hostess gifts, jewelry, painted floorcloths, sachets, flower arrangements, lamp shades, and paper. Children take classes in drawing and painting, as well as making lip gloss and bubble bath. "Nothing," says Lisa, "is more special than giving people a part of yourself." Classes are taught by Lisa, by an employee, or by an outside expert. Adult students, who bring their own food and wine, pay for the classes, and teachers receive half of the revenue from the evening.

For Lisa, as for many other women, the hardest part of having a store is "balancing the money—paying people generously, giving customers the most for their dollar, and paying my own bills." The best part of her business is doing weddings and other big parties. "I ask a ton of questions and let the people talk, so I know exactly what they're visualizing," she explains. "Making that into reality is what I love. I enjoy making people happy and sharing in whatever occasion they are having in their life."

Crafts classes, held at an informal worktable, are a natural part of Out of Hand. "Flowers and handcrafted items were the start of the business" says Lisa. "All the other ideas just grew from that."

CREATING DEMAND

Kate's Paperie

KATE FLAX

hen Kate Flax opened the first Kate's Paperie, she was already a savvy businesswoman. She had spent years working as a manager and troubleshooter for the Manhattan art supply stores her husband's family had started early in the twentieth century. But she wanted a shop of her own. So she showed her husband a business plan; its main concept was the selling of fancy wrapping papers displayed so shoppers could flip through them the way they flipped through wallpaper books. Her husband agreed that New York City might get as excited as she was about a "wonderful and amazing paper shop." It turns out that Kate's timing was perfect. In the computer-driven late 1980s, people were longing for handwritten letters, invitations, journals, and diaries.

The delicate-looking "wedding cake" is an example of Kate's extraordinary gift-wrapping service. Any paper sold in the store can be purchased by the sheet and used to wrap a gift, even if it doesn't come from the shop. Standard house wrap, incorporating three pleats in the paper (an uneven number for happy occasions, according to Japanese tsutsumu tradition) and tied with raffia, is free.

Kate's Paperie offerings are so bountiful and beautiful they could serve as both art and the inspiration for artful writing. There is wrapping tissue embedded with gold leaf, notepaper inlaid with rose petals, silky rice paper from Thailand, marbleized papers and journals, gold mesh decorative boxes, glassine sheets for preserving dried flowers, and special boxes for storing photographs. Her shops carry forty thousand different papers, all in touchable hanging displays and all available by the individual sheet. And in case this selection isn't enough, Kate's offers courses in papermaking, as well as gift wrapping and the use of sealing wax.

Each store has a different personality depending on its location. The first, in Greenwich Village, has an arty, accessible ambience that makes neighboring university and art students feel at home. With the second store, a 7,000-square-foot space in a landmark building in SoHo, Kate admits it took her a while to put together the right mix of merchandise to appeal to the trendy area's young people, tourists, and serious artists. "We went through a transition," she says, "and I made errors. But if you don't make errors, you don't grow. The idea is not to repeat them."

Although this lily of the valley "tree" looks as if its blossoms had just been picked, they're actually another example of the way Kate's turns paper into art. Photo albums and writing journals complete the display.

In 1998 she opened a store in a 6,000-square-foot former pharmacy on the Upper East Side and got it right on the first try. She immediately began reaching out to local families by providing chairs, drawing pads, and an artist to keep children occupied while their parents shopped. Sometimes, says Kate, there are forty strollers in the store—and everyone is calm and happy.

Kate knows that one of the secrets to making sales, especially for gifts, is walking customers around the store and offering suggestions as you go. She makes sure her staff gives that kind of personal attention to shoppers—the same kind of attention, in fact, that Kate gives to her employees. "If you dig a little deeper," she says, "the potential is there: A light bulb comes on and they begin to blossom."

The Paperie's wrappings, sometimes bound with as many as four layers of sumptuous ribbon and bouquets of faux flowers (opposite), seem too lovely to open, but Kate encourages handling the wares. The shop also offers photographic restoration services (below).

Two Shops of Her Own

Nell Hill's and G. Diebolts

MARY CAROL GARRITY

Mary Carol Garrity has always loved retail. From the age of ten, she spent many spare moments in her father's clothing store in Atchison, Kansas, a town of about eight thousand long past its glory days as the seat of the Atchison, Topeka & Santa Fe Railroad. Fifteen years after that earliest selling experience, she opened a small gourmet shop and named it Nell Hill's for her grandmother. But Atchison was too small to support the shop, even when Mary Carol added kitchen gadgets and appliances to the merchandise mix. After a seven-year evolution from food to furniture, home decor, and home accessories, she found her niche. Nell Hill's now draws shoppers from miles around with a mix of antiques and new pieces, bought at furniture fairs and antiques

In the mid-1990s, Mary Carol, already owner of the wildly popular Nell Hill's, tripled her retail space when she purchased a ninety-year-old bank. She turned it into a bed and bath linens shop and named it G. Diebolts, after her father's store.

G. DIEBOLTS
CUSTOM BEDDING & LINENS

dealers in the United States and Europe and shown in unpredictable pairings. Mary Carol might place a $12 finial on an expensive antique library desk; layer accessories such as jars, trays, candles, and tassels on simple tables; and pile on the pillows, pictures, and mirrors—all with so much subtlety and taste that the crowded array never looks overdone.

At G. Diebolts, feminine touches such as appliquéd quilts and tasseled pillows harmonize surprisingly well with the former bank's vaulted ceilings and turn-of-the-century light fixtures.

Mary Carol considers flexibility a key to her success. She never invests a lot in any one type of inventory, and when she sees that something isn't selling, she has no hesitation

about replacing it with something different. "It's a store that reinvents its look every year," says Mary Carol. This reputation for change brings people back to Atchison on a regular basis to see what's new. It also encourages them to buy an item when they see it, since it will probably be gone by the time they return.

What makes Nell Hill's an entertainment draw is not just its nicely honed mix of pieces but also the feeling of warmth Mary Carol and her staff of at least thirty bring to the shopping experience. Mary Carol is in the store during most of its business hours and on the floor dealing with customers 99 percent of that time. She has neither an office nor a desk; she returns her calls from work or home after the store closes. Her interaction with customers begins with a greeting, but it doesn't end there. She thinks of herself as running an eight-hour cocktail party, and as people move around the store's enormous and tightly packed selection of merchandise, they naturally begin chatting and the store becomes amazingly friendly. Everyone wants to be in on the good time, which is obviously genuine, because, as Mary Carol says, "We couldn't fake it as many hours a day as we do it."

Mary Carol stocks a wide range of fabrics, ruffles, and bedskirts. She also sells custom pillows and quilts; because the work is done locally, prices are sometimes lower than for ready-made.

The overwhelming majority of Nell Hill's customers drive at least an hour and a quarter each way to get to the shop; many are from as far away as Omaha and Kansas City, each hours away. Employees know them by their first names, and because they recall what shoppers purchased in the past, they're able to give helpful decorating tips.

Mary Carol doesn't always wait for customers to make the trip to her. She tries to drum up new business by going to high-end charity bazaars in cities where she doesn't yet have a following. Here, she entices new shoppers by presenting a "killer" booth crammed with great pieces at great prices. Pretty soon the bazaar customers are making the trip to Atchison—and bringing their friends with them.

Because Mary Carol understands the way her customers live, Christmas decorations begin appearing in the store as early as August and are "over the top" by the first of October. Customers can be done with their shopping by the end of November, leaving them time to spend with family and friends as the holidays approach.

She also understands the lives of her employees and is willing to be as flexible with them as she is in finding the right mix of merchandise. A parent can come to work early and leave early to be home when her child gets out of school; if a two-day work week suits an employee, Mary Carol will try to accommodate him. "It must be as good for them as it is for me to work here," she says. She promotes the attitude that

Along with two dozen chairs, a dozen sofas, and a wealth of fabric choices, Nell Hill's main floor also displays European antiques and garden objects. Casual dishes and other tabletop accessories are displayed on the second level.

GARDENERS
SALAD
TOMATO
GIANT DELICIOUS
TOMATO
YELLOW JUBILEE
LOW IN ACID
$1.00
BEAN
ROMANO ITALIAN POLE
69¢
EGGPLANT
BLACK BEAUTY
89¢
POTS
TEA

everyone in the store has to help everyone else, and she has never asked anyone to do what she herself wouldn't do, including vacuuming and taking out the trash.

Mary Carol's other store, called G. Diebolts, is also in Atchison. It's a quieter place than Nell Hill's, which is quite appropriate, as it sells furniture and accessories for the quiet activities of the day—sleeping and bathing. Even with the success of Nell Hill's as a guide, it took four years for G. Diebolts to take off.

In early 2001, when it seemed as if the buoyant economy of the 1990s was slipping, Mary Carol asked her manufacturers' representatives how the big department stores were coping. Told they were holding back, she bought as if there was no tomorrow, both to show her optimism in the face of a possible downturn and because it would allow her to offer inventory other stores couldn't provide. "It was a huge risk," she explains, "but it paid off. We had a lot of merchandise, but we needed it.

"When a national chain opens up nearby, some people think it's an excuse to fail," she continues. "I see it as an opportunity to strut our stuff and give all the service we can. People really value their time, and for many shopping is also entertainment. If they're having a good time, they'll spend their money." Customers spend millions of dollars a year in Mary Carol's stores. And everyone is having fun.

Mary Carol is continually redecorating her stores—setting and resetting the stage—to keep things fresh for her customers and to fill in where purchases have been made.

Let Your Business Grow

Linda Campisano Millinery

LINDA CAMPISANO

inda Campisano was designing clothes for Barbie dolls when she was six. She didn't turn her talent to making luxurious hats for real women until she had become the mother of five and earned a degree from the Art Institute of Chicago, in that order. She now sells her creations in a large studio in a quaint section of the Chicago suburb of Evanston, where she lives, and in a modern, minimalist-looking boutique in the swank 900 North Michigan mall in downtown Chicago.

She began making and selling hats in a workshop in her basement, and got her first big break when one of her hats appeared in the idiosyncratic, refined (and now defunct) J. Peterman catalog, which gave her just a month to make five hundred hats. The money from

This building in Evanston perfectly evoked an era when wearing hats was de rigueur. Linda and her husband renovated the space themselves. They brought it up to modern retailing standards but kept its architectural integrity and period charm.

Linda Campisano
Millinery
Millinery

Linda Campisano
Chicago, Illinois
Linda Campisano
Chicago, Illinois
Linda Campisano
Chicago, Illinois

that sale gave her the capital to open a small shop in Evanston.

Because she and her husband were willing to do the renovations on her Evanston space themselves, Linda was able to negotiate a reduction in rent. She did the same at 900 North Michigan after the mall owner invited her to locate there. The latter is in a spot that has given her access to the many Hollywood people, including costume designers, who stay in the mall's Four Seasons Hotel. Her customers include Steve Martin and Helena Bonham Carter, as well as Senator Hillary Rodham Clinton.

Linda's second break was a purchase she made from a couple who owned a renowned millinery shop near the Art Institute: an "archaeological dig" containing five thousand antique hat blocks. The collection was so varied and unusual that the Smithsonian Institution has expressed interest in displaying them. This bounty, which took weeks to "excavate," also included priceless trim such as 1950s Christian Dior roses from Paris and swan feathers from the 1920s, which Linda uses, along with selected molds and hat blocks, as decoration for her Evanston studio.

Not long after she started, Linda ran into trouble when a venture capitalist friend said he would finance the growth of her business if she would bring out a perfume. This turned out to be a painful and expensive diversion from her true calling as a milliner

The merchandise display in Linda's North Michigan Mall shop reflects a mix of modern and traditional styles. A clean, architectural arrangement of hats on elegant hat stands is coupled with a row of simple, dramatic hat boxes.

and left Linda with serious debt. When she couldn't pay her vendors, she was honest about her situation, kept them up to date on her progress in paying down the debt, and asked for longer payment terms. They agreed because of her good performance in the past.

With her intuition about personality and an artist's eye, Linda makes sure her customers' hats are as flattering as a good haircut. And because she understands that shopping is often a form of rejuvenation, she goes out of her way to make a shopper feel "like a goddess." Whether the customer is buying a $50 silk flower or a $500 hat, she feels comfortable shopping for as long as she likes and is offered tea, coffee, Champagne, and chocolate truffles. In addition to her everyday hospitality, Linda offers Tuesdays with Tea and Thursdays with Hot Chocolate at the Michigan Avenue store. She uses these occasions to network with other shop owners when business is slow.

Linda has also used her artistic talent to make elaborate one-of-a-kind business cards and stationery. She believes her distinctive graphics have been more effective publicity than advertising space purchased in magazines and newspapers.

Linda and her family unearthed these hat blocks in the basement of a famous millinery store in downtown Chicago. She purchased them for $20,000 so she could carry on the hat-making tradition. The collection lines an eighteen-foot wall in the Evanston shop.

Her biggest reward is seeing people happy when they go home with the "perfect" hat. It may be for a special celebration; it may

be a much-needed tonic in bad times: Linda designs hats for cancer patients and often receives heartfelt notes of appreciation for her time and effort in helping them. She also hears from the women who live in a retirement home near the downtown Chicago store. Making their way to the shop on a regular basis, their eyes light up when they arrive. "Linda, you can never close," they tell her. "We look forward to seeing what you have in the window every day."

Both custom and ready-to-wear pieces are made by hand in dozens of colors. A wide variety of trims, including vintage ribbon and silk flowers, are available.

Global Expansion

Eileen Fisher

EILEEN FISHER

ileen Fisher was a graphic artist in New York with a background in interior design who resented the need to keep up with fashion and wanted to be able to dress as simply as men do. In 1984, a jeweler friend offered her the chance to sell her own women's clothing designs from his booth at an industry trade show. Using her savings of $350, she created four mix-and-match pieces—a tunic, a wide-leg pant, a vest, and a shell—took them to the show, and went home with $3,000 in orders. Three months later, at another show, with eight pieces, she did $40,000 worth of business. At a third show, the orders totaled an astounding $90,000.

The four original pieces from the first collection, slightly modified, are still available under the name "Essentials." New collections are added each season in fabric- and color-coordinated groupings.

By then Eileen had several employees and had moved her business from the downtown loft where she lived to a warehouse nearby

and applied for a bank loan. When it was turned down, she put her creativity to work: She borrowed money from friends at 2 percent a month, repaying it in the three months it took her to fill orders. She also got friends to pay in advance for clothes she sold them at wholesale prices.

Although her separates can be put together in many ways—like Lego pieces, she says—an Eileen Fisher outfit has a recognizable look. The lines are fluid and forgiving of figure flaws, often with elasticized waists. They're made of high-quality, solid-color fabrics in natural fibers; flat knits and linens are favorites. Unadorned, with closures either concealed or nonexistent, the pieces have an Asian sensibility. True to her vision of good-looking practicality, the fabrics are likely to be washable; pieces from one season coordinate with pieces from another; and sizes now include Petite and Women's, together accounting for 20 percent of her sales.

Eileen opened her first shop in the East Village in 1987, where her classic looks were in stark contrast to the pink hair and torn jeans of the area's denizens. In 1991, with her husband in charge of the retail side of the business, she opened a second store in midtown Manhattan. There are now twenty-five Eileen Fisher stores throughout the country, all modern and airy so the clothing can take center stage. Her clothes are also carried in nearly one thousand specialty shops and thirteen department store chains from Canada to Kuwait. She is the 80 percent owner of a business that grew at the rate of 35 to 45 percent in the mid-1990s. In the fickle fashion industry, she is a phenomenon.

She's also mindful of the world in which she lives. In 1999 her company donated 3 percent of its pretax profits to charitable organizations, and hired a manager of social accountability to look after human rights in the factories that produce her clothing around the world.

Fabric swatch cards are created for new lines each season, allowing sales associates and shoppers to anticipate and plan wardrobe additions together. Corresponding watercolor renderings of new monthly offerings bring the clothing to life.

THE LEARNING CURVE

La Knitterie Parisienne

EDITH EIG

Edith Eig learned to knit as a five-year-old schoolgirl in Paris, so it isn't surprising that she teaches knitting to children at La Knitterie Parisienne, her cornucopia of yarns and accessories in Studio City, California. Some of her students are as young as six—"Most children master technique very quickly, some in less than an hour, and learn coordination and patience in the process," she explains. They make hats, dolls, teddy bears, place mats, purses, and even armbands for school sports teams. Edith feels it's important that the parents know how to knit as well, so that children with questions won't be frustrated.

Accompanying their mothers to the shop, many children are intrigued enough by the brightly colored skeins to try knitting themselves. Edith uses a little word picture to teach them how to use needles and yarn: "Go to the front door, around the tree, down the basement, and off you go."

Edith also teaches adult classes on Tuesdays, when the shop is closed, and provides a

anny blatt

kind of old-fashioned sewing circle for up to twenty-four people on Wednesday nights and Saturdays, during store hours. This kind of gathering is "especially important in California, where everyone is from somewhere else and people are looking for a home away from home," she says. Classes are free, even though some of Edith's competition charges $25, but participants are required to buy their supplies from La Knitterie Parisienne.

Taking her knitting skills on the road, Edith gives lessons at baby showers, teaching guests how to make squares to be assembled into a baby blanket, and at malls, where knitting is billed as a major way to reduce stress.

But people come to La Knitterie Parisienne for more than lessons. A master knitter, Edith displays and sells her haute couture women's sweaters and accessories—hats, scarves, gloves, purses, and shawls—as well as baby sweaters and crib blankets, to inspire both knitters and shoppers. She uses honesty—"the biggest tool you can have"—tempered with tact and diplomacy to steer shoppers toward flattering styles and colors.

The motto of La Knitterie Parisienne is "Come as a stranger, leave as a friend." This applies to staff as well: Employees, who must have excellent knitting skills and easygoing personalities, love being part of the spiritual aura that permeates the shop. One worker retired to Italy, only to move back to California because she missed the store's conviviality.

Edith has spread that spirit across the country. In the aftermath of the September 11 terrorist attacks on New York City's World Trade Center, she put together an afghan with squares knitted by celebrities and auctioned it on eBay to benefit the New York Police & Fire Widows' and Children's Benefit Fund.

Edith offers her knitters a huge selection of buttons—designer, porcelain, vintage, and semiprecious stone—along with a mouthwatering array of colorful yarns from all over the world.

Edna Mae's
Millinery
The Aesthetic
Accessory
3 Cook St., P.O. Box
Washington, CT 06
(860) 868-28

RESOURCES

VICTORIA

Victoria magazine regularly features inspirational articles on women who have opened successful businesses of all kinds, including retail shops. The Victoria web site (www.victoriamag.com) features a section devoted to entrepreneurship, and offers invaluable business advice, including start-up tips and lists of useful small business organizations, associations, and agencies. For *Victoria* subscriptions call (515) 283-2578 or visit the *Victoria* web site.

BOOKS

Business Basics: A Microbusiness Startup Guide, by Gerard Dodd (Central Point, Oregon: Oasis Press/PSI Research, 1998).
Drawings, charts, and sample forms make this book extremely user-friendly. While not aimed specifically at retail businesses, what it has to say about finances, competition, and people will benefit retailers as well as others.

The Entrepreneur Magazine Small Business Advisor (New York: John Wiley & Sons, 1999).
No-nonsense approach to information required for all small businesses. Although many of the businesses discussed are large compared to a single retail store, this volume is useful because of the breadth of its coverage.

Guerrilla Marketing: Secrets for Making Big Profits From Your Small Business by Jay Conrad Levinson (Boston: Houghton Mifflin, 1998).
This update of the 1983 revolutionary book on marketing defines strategies and provides workable, low-cost ideas, including how to use modern technology to attract and keep customers.

Retail in Detail: How to Start and Manage a Small Retail Business by Ronald L. Bond (Central Point, Oregon: Oasis Press/PSI Research, 2001).
Bond and his wife have owned three different retail businesses in the South and Midwest. This practical and straightforward book tells you all you need to know to follow in their footsteps, and illustrates general points with their actual experiences.

So You Want to Own the Store: Secrets to Running a Successful Retail Operation by Mort Brown and Thomas Tilling (Chicago: Contemporary Books, 1997).
A wonderful book filled with readable, down-to-earth advice, real-life examples, and detailed appendices.

Specialty Shop Retailing: How to Run Your Own Store by Carol L. Schroeder (New York: John Wiley & Sons, 1997).
This guide, written by a woman who owns several large kitchen equipment and tabletop stores, helps you avoid employee and customer problems. Good glossary and bibliography.

Working Solo Sourcebook: Essential Resources for Independent Entrepreneurs by Terri Lonier (New York: John Wiley & Sons, 1998).
This book lists 1,200 business resources for more than 40 different fields, including helpful government agencies, publications, educational programs, and professional associations.

MAGAZINES

Accessories
New York, NY
(212) 686-4412
Trends, hot sellers, previews and calendars useful for shops selling socks and stockings, rainwear, bridal accessories, and handbags. Special section on what appeals to juniors, who are big buyers of accessories.

Earnshaw's Infants, Girls & Boys Wear Review
Babylon, NY
(631) 661-4637
Trends, market reports, trade show calendars, and sources make this a useful magazine for sellers of upscale children's clothing.

Entrepreneur: Solutions for Growing Businesses
Irvine, CA
(800)274-6229
www.entrepreneur.com
Practical publication with sections devoted to money, management, women, government assistance, and public policy issues.

Gifts & Dec
(Gifts & Decorative Accessories)
New York, NY
(212) 519-7200
www.GiftsandDec.com.
Trends, predictions, management advice, and inspiration, as well as information on trade shows and new products for retailers of gifts and decorative accessories.

ASSOCIATIONS AND ORGANIZATIONS

Canadian Association of Women Executives & Entrepreneurs (CAWEE),
3 Church Street, Suite 604
Toronto, ON M5E 1M2
Canada
(416) 756-0000
www.cawee.net
CAWEE offers monthly events, including workshops, conferences, and speakers; meets with national and international businesswomen's groups; and stages trade shows annually, including ones devoted to women's global business concerns.

The Entrepreneurship Institute
3592 Corporate Drive, Suite 101
Columbus, OH 43231
(614) 895-1153
www.tei.net
Provides resources for the expansion of small and medium-size businesses. Business owners, bankers, accountants, attorneys, and investors make up advisory boards that offer educational and networking programs.

National Association of Women Business Owners (NAWBO)
1595 Spring Hill Road, Suite 330
Vienna, VA 22182
(703) 506-3268
www.nawbo.org
With more than 60 chapters, this association represents the interests of women entrepreneurs in all types of businesses. It is affiliated with Les Femmes Chefs d'Entreprises Mondiales (World Association of Women Entrepreneurs). Online services include information on business magazines, business and industry resources, and international links to associations like the Canadian Women's Business Network and Women-Connect-Asia.

Service Corps of Retired Executives (SCORE)
(800) 634-0245
www.score.org
An arm of the SBA, SCORE is dedicated to aiding in the formation, growth, and success of small businesses nationwide. SCORE matches volunteers experienced in business with current and prospective business owners in need of expert advice in every area of business. SCORE maintains a national skills bank to identify the best counselors for its clients.

Small Business Administration (SBA)
409 3rd Street, SW, 4th Floor
Washington, DC, 20416
(800) 827-5722
www.sba.gov
SBA is an invaluable U.S. government organization providing information on many topics, including how to seek capital, how to comply with tax codes, where to find advice, how to develop your business, and how to manage growth. SBA publishes The Small Business Resource Guide, *which lists sources of assistance for small businesses in the federal, state, and private sectors. General inquiries about SBA services and resources available from federal, state, and local government agencies should be directed to the Small Business Answer Desk at the number listed above.*

U.S. Chamber of Commerce
1615 H Street, NW
Washington, DC 20062
(202) 659-6000
www.uschamber.org
The U.S. Chamber of Commerce, working with local and state chambers, represents national business interests to the federal government. It publishes many guides, including The Small Business Financial Resource Guide. *Local chambers run programs on small business start-up and development, counsel on small business problems, and provide start-up assistance, lending, and equity capital programs.*

SOFTWARE

Excellent accounting programs, for the management of both personal and small business finances, include Quicken, QuickBooks, QuickBooks Pro, Microsoft Money, and Peachtree.

WEB SITES

www.onlinewbc.gov
The site of the Women's Business Centers of the SBA. It gives practical information geared to women entrepreneurs, tutorials, downloadable forms, basic accounting, inspiration, and practical advice on such topics as networking, business basics, and local services. The site is in five languages in addition to English.

www.startupbiz.com
A site offering expert advice via free articles on the Internet, referrals to experts, and a store selling books and templates helpful to shop owners.

www.victoriamag.com
Click on *Entrepreneur Workshop* for concrete tools, networking possibilities, and inspirational stories. Downloadable templates for business plans, income statements, and other financial forms.

Business Directory

Anandamali
Cheryl Hazan
35 North Moore Street
New York, NY 10013
(212) 343-8964
www.anandamali.com

Angel Heart
Nina Kaplan
10 South State Street
Newtown, PA 18940
(215) 968-1614

Anne Fontaine
Anne Fontaine
(866) AF-SHIRT
www.annefontaine.com

Barefoot Contessa
Ina Garten
46 Newtown Lane
East Hampton, NY 11937
(800) 844-7002
www.barefootcontessa.com

Dancing Deer Baking Company, Inc.
Trish Karter
77 Shirley Street
Boston, MA 02119
(888) 699-3337
www.dancingdeer.com

Desana
Paula and Karen Goldstein
46 Waltham Street
Courtyard
Boston, MA 02118
(617) 556-0077
www.desana.com

Devonia
Lori Hedtler
43 Charles Street
Boston, MA 02114
(617) 523-8313
www.devonia-antiques.com

Eileen Fisher
Eileen Fisher
(800) 345-3362
www.eileenfisher.com

Eleish–van Breems Antiques
Rhonda Eleish and
Edie van Breems
Thompson House
487 Main Street South
Woodbury, CT 06798
(203) 263-7030
www.evbantiques.com

Elyssa B Designs
Elyssa Silbert
9061 Nemo Street
West Hollywood, CA
90069
(310) 273-6860

Farmhouse
Eileen Main
Shaftsbury, VT
(802) 440-9688
www.farmhouseonline.com

Fino Fino
Carolyn Busch
325 Sharon Park Drive
Menlo Park, CA 94025
(650) 854-8030
www.finofino.com

Flower Hardware
Cecelia Heffernan
3445 North Pines Way
Wilson, WY 83014
(307) 733-7040
www.flowerhardware.com

Flowers by Cecelia
Cecelia Heffernan
(307) 733-0423

Flowers by Michéle
Michéle Rosier
500 Broadway
Santa Monica, CA 90401
(310) 656-0688

Fraiche
Lorraine Eastman
8361 West 3rd Street
Los Angeles, CA 90048
(888) 654-7002
www.fraichegifts.com

French General
Kaari and Molly Meng
35 Crosby Street
New York, NY 10013
(212) 343-7474
www.frenchgeneral.com

French Lace
Nina Kaplan
17 South State Street
Newtown, PA 18940
(215) 579-6956
www.frenchlace.com

G. Diebolts
Mary Carol Garrity
608 Commercial
Atchison, KS 66002
(913) 367-2395

Grandmother's Buttons
Susan Davis
PO Box 1689
9814 Royal Street
St. Francisville, LA 70775
(225) 635-4107

Grasmere
Beth Siqueland-Gresch
40 Maple Avenue
Barrington, RI 02806
(401) 247-2789
www.grasmeretheshop.com

Henry's General Store
Maura Koutoujian
PO Box 34
604 West Water Street
Princeton, WI 54968
(888) 7-HENRYS
www.henrysgeneralstore.com

Jo Malone
Jo Malone
949 Broadway
New York, NY 10011
(212) 673-2220

Judy Green's Garden Shop
Judy Green
London, England
011 44 207 435 3832

Judy Pascal Antiques
Judy Pascal
Le Depôt
PO Box 106
145 Elm Street
Manchester Center, VT 05255
(802) 362-2004

Kate's Paperie
Kate Flax
561 Broadway
New York, NY 10012
(212) 941-9816
www.katespaperie.com

La Knitterie Parisienne
Edith Eig
12642 Ventura Boulevard
Studio City, CA 91604
(818) 766-1515
www.laknitterieparisienne.com

Liberty
Wendy Williams-Watt
1295 Seymour Street
Vancouver, BC V6B 3N6
Canada
(604) 682-7499

Linda Campisano Millinery
Linda Campisano
522 Davis Street
Evanston, IL 60202
(847) 475-7565
900 North Michagan Avenue, 6th Floor
Chicago, IL 60610
(312) 337-1004

Linda Getchell's
Linda Getchell
5012 Xerxes Avenue South
Minneapolis, MN 55410
(612) 922-6222

London Lace
Diane Loesch Jones
215 Newbury Street
Boston, MA 02116
(800) 926-5223
www.londonlace.com

Maiden Lane
Shirley Maiden
Le Depôt
PO Box 106
145 Elm Street
Manchester Center, VT 05255
(802) 362-2004

The McCharles House
Audrey and Vivian Heredia
335 South C Street
Tustin, CA 92780
(714) 731-4063
www.mccharleshouse.com

Nell Hill's
Mary Carol Garrity
501 Commercial
Atchison, KS 66002
(913) 367-1086
www.nellhills.com

Nest Feathers
Neva Scott
301 Wellsian Way
Richland, WA 99352
(509) 943-3374
www.nestfeathers.com

Out of Hand
Lisa Wofford
113C Pitt Street
Mt. Pleasant, SC 29464
(843) 856-3585
www.artofcreating.com

Pamela Scurry's Wicker Garden's Baby
Pamela Scurry
1327 Madison Ave.
New York, NY 10128
(212) 348-1166
www.wickergarden.com

Papyrus
Dominique Schurman
(707) 425-8006
www.papyrusonline.com

Peacock Alley
Mary Ella Gabler
334 East 59th Street
New York, NY 10022
(800) 496-2880
3210 Armstrong Avenue
Dallas, TX 75205
(800) 652-3818
www.peacockalley.com

Peggy Jean's Pies
Peggy Day and Jeanne Wagster
1605 Chapel Hill
Columbia, MO 65203
(573) 447-1119
www.peggyjeanspies.com

Peter Beaton Hat Studio
Darcy Creech
16½ Federal Street
Nantucket, MA 02554
(888) 723-2866
www.peterbeaton.com

Putti Fine Furnishings
Linda Wade
1104 Yonge Street
Toronto, ON M4W2L6
Canada
(800) 649-3120
(416) 972-7652

Room with a View
Elizabeth Lamont
1600 Montana Ave.
Santa Monica, CA 90403
(800) 410-9175
www.roomview.com

Spruce
Gaige Clark
75 Greenwich Avenue
New York, NY 10014
(212) 414-0588
www.spruceup.com

StoneKelly
Jen Stone and Don Kelly
641 West 59th Street
New York, NY 10019
(212) 245-6611
www.stonekelly.com

Suzanne's Millinery
Suzanne Newman
27 East 61st Street
New York, NY 10021
(212) 593-3232

Ta Da!
Rosie Daykin
2308 West Broadway
Vancouver, BC V6K 2E5
Canada
(604) 736-3011

Wild Thyme
Laurie deGrazia
5725 Kennett Pike
Centerville, DE 19807
(302) 656-4454

Photo Credits

1	William P. Steele
2	Jeff McNamara
7–8	Toshi Otsuki
10	Gross & Daley (top) Michael Weschler (bottom)
12	Toshi Otsuki
17	Alan Weintraub
18	Robert Melnychuk
22	Michael Weschler
26	Kit Latham
30–31	Gross & Daley
34	William P. Steele
36–37	Toshi Otsuki
38–45	Robert Melnychuk
46–53	Jeff McNamara
54–58	Gross & Daley
60–65	Toshi Otsuki
66–72	Susan Gentry McWhinney
74–79	Robert Melnychuk
80	Dominique Vorillon (top) Toshi Otsuki (bottom)
82	Steven Randazzo
87	Toshi Otsuki
89	Gross & Daley
90	Bryan McCay
93	Toshi Otsuki
97	Luciana Pampalone
98–101	Toshi Otsuki
102	Jeff McNamara
104–105	Toshi Otsuki
106	William P. Steele
108	Toshi Otsuki
109	Robert Melnychuk
110–111	Hedrich Blessing
114	Gross & Daley
118–123	Toshi Otsuki
124–129	Luciana Pampalone
130–136	Langdon Clay
138–145	Gross & Daley
146	Jana Taylor (top) William P. Steele (bottom)
148	Pia Tryde
152–164	Toshi Otsuki
166	Jeff McNamara
169	Toshi Otsuki
170–177	Michael Skott
178–182	Gross & Daley
184–189	Toshi Otsuki
190–198	William P. Steele
200–207	Hedrich Blessing
208–210	Toshi Otsuki
212–214	Jana Taylor
216	Steven Randazzo
224	Toshi Otsuki

INK